Tampa Bay Rays 2020

A Baseball Companion

Edited by R.J. Anderson, Craig Goldstein and Bret Sayre

Baseball Prospectus

Craig Brown, Steven Goldman and David Pease, Consultant Editors
Robert Au, Harry Pavlidis and Amy Pircher, Statistics Editors

Copyright © 2020 by DIY Baseball, LLC.
All rights reserved

This book or any part thereof may not be reproduced or transmitted in any form or by any means, electronic or mechanical, including photocopying, recording, or by any information storage and retrieval system, without permission in writing from the publisher.

Limit of Liability/Disclaimer of Warranty: While the publisher and the author have used their best efforts in preparing this book, they make no representations or warranties with respect to the accuracy or completeness of the contents of this book and specifically disclaim any implied warranties of merchantability or fitness for a particular purpose. No warranty may be created or extended by sales representatives or written sales materials. The advice and strategies contained herein may not be suitable for your situation. You should consult with a professional where appropriate. Neither the publisher nor the author shall be liable for any loss of profit or any other commercial damages, including but not limited to special, incidental, consequential, or other damages.

Library of Congress Cataloging-in-Publication Data:
paperback
ISBN-13: 978-1-949332-88-9

Project Credits
Cover Design: Michael Byzewski at Aesthetic Apparatus
Interior Design and Production: Jeff Pease, Dave Pease
Layout: Jeff Pease, Dave Pease

Baseball icon courtesy of Uberux, from https://www.shareicon.net/author/uberux

Ballpark diagram courtesy of Lou Spirito/THIRTY81 Project, https://thirty81project.com/

Manufactured in the United States of America
10 9 8 7 6 5 4 3 2 1

Table of Contents

Statistical Introduction v

Part 1: Team Analysis

Tampa Bay Rays: Where Are You Going, Where Have You Been? 3
    Scott Orgera and Matthew Trueblood

Performance Graphs 9

2019 Team Performance 10

2020 Team Projections 11

Team Personnel 12

Tropicana Field Stats 13

Rays Team Analysis 15

Part 2: Player Analysis

Rays Player Analysis 26

Rays Prospects 103

Part 3: Featured Articles

The Baseball Is Juiced (Again) 119
    Robert Arthur

The Moral Hazard of Playing It Safe 123
    Craig Goldstein

Index of Names 129

Statistical Introduction

Sports are, fundamentally, a blend of athletic endeavor and storytelling. Baseball, like any other sport, tells its stories in so many ways: in the arc of a game from the stands or a season from the box scores, in photos, or even in numbers. At Baseball Prospectus, we understand that statistics don't replace observation or any of baseball's stories, but complement everything else that makes the game so much fun.

What stats help us with is with patterns and precision, variance and value. This book can help you learn things you may not see from watching a game or hundred, whether it's the path of a career over time or the breadth of the entire MLB. We'd also never ask you to choose between our numbers and the experience of viewing a game from the cheap seats or the comfort of your home; our publication combines running the numbers with observations and wisdom from some of the brightest minds we can find. But if you *do* want to learn more about the numbers beyond what's on the backs of player jerseys, let us help explain.

Offense

We've revised our methodology for determining batting value. Long-time readers of the book will notice that we've retired True Average in favor of a new metric: Deserved Runs Created Plus (DRC+). Developed by Jonathan Judge and our stats team, this statistic measures everything a player does at the plate–reaching base, hitting for power, making outs, and moving runners over–and puts it on a scale where 100 equals league-average performance. A DRC+ of 150 is terrific, a DRC+ of 100 is average and a DRC+ of 75 means you better be an excellent defender.

DRC+ also does a better job than any of our previous metrics in taking contextual factors into account. The model adjusts for how the park affects performance, but also for things like the talent of the opposing pitcher, value of different types of batted-ball events, league, temperature and other factors. It's able to describe a player's expected offensive contribution than any other statistic we've found over the years, and also does a better job of predicting future performance as well.

There's a lot more to DRC+'s story, and you can read all about it in greater depth near the end of this book.

The other aspect of run-scoring is baserunning, which we quantify using Baserunning Runs. BRR not only records the value of stolen bases (or getting caught in the act), but also accounts for all the stuff that doesn't show up on the back of a baseball card: a runner's ability to go first to third on a single, or advance on a fly ball.

Defense

Where offensive value is *relatively* easy to identify and understand, defensive value is...not. Over the past dozen years, the sabermetric community has focused mostly on stats based on zone data: a real-live human person records the type of batted ball and estimated landing location, and models are created that give expected outs. From there, you can compare fielders' actual outs to those expected ones. Simple, right?

Unfortunately, zone data has two major issues. First, zone data is recorded by commercial data providers who keep the raw data private unless you pay for it. (All the statistics we build in this book and on our website use public data as inputs.) That hurts our ability to test assumptions or duplicate results. Second, over the years it has become apparent that there's quite a bit of "noise" in zone-based fielding analysis. Sometimes the conclusions drawn from zone data don't hold up to scrutiny, and sometimes the different data provided by different providers don't look anything alike, giving wildly different results. Sometimes the hard-working professional stringers or scorers might unknowingly inflict unconscious bias into the mix: for example good fielders will often be credited with more expected outs despite the data, and ballparks with high press boxes tend to score more line drives than ones with a lower press box.

Enter our Fielding Runs Above Average (FRAA). For most positions, FRAA is built from play-by-play data, which allows us to avoid the subjectivity found in many other fielding metrics. The idea is this: count how many fielding plays are made by a given player and compare that to expected plays for an average fielder at their position (based on pitcher ground ball tendencies and batter handedness). Then we adjust for park and base-out situations.

When it comes to catchers, our methodology is a little different thanks to the laundry list of responsibilities they're tasked with beyond just, well, catching and throwing the ball. By now you've probably heard about "framing" or the art of making umpires more likely to call balls outside the strike zone for strikes. To put this into one tidy number, we incorporate pitch tracking data (for the years it exists) and adjust for important factors like pitcher, umpire, batter and home-field advantage using a mixed-model approach. This grants us a number for how many strikes the catcher is personally adding to (or subtracting from) his pitchers' performance...which we then convert to runs added or lost using linear weights.

Framing is one of the biggest parts of determining catcher value, but we also take into account blocking balls from going past, whether a scorer deems it a passed ball or a wild pitch. We use a similar approach—one that really benefits from the pitch tracking data that tells us what ends up in the dirt and what doesn't. We also include a catcher's ability to prevent stolen bases and how well they field balls in play, and *finally* we come up with our FRAA for catchers.

Pitching

Both pitching and fielding make up the half of baseball that isn't run scoring: run prevention. Separating pitching from fielding is a tough task, and most recent pitching analysis has branched off from Voros McCracken's famous (and controversial) statement, "There is little if any difference among major-league pitchers in their ability to prevent hits on balls hit in the field of play." The research of the analytic community has validated this to some extent, and there are a host of "defense-independent" pitching measures that have been developed to try and extract the effect of the defense behind a hurler from the pitcher's work.

Our solution to this quandary is Deserved Run Average (DRA), our core pitching metric. DRA looks like earned run average (ERA), the tried-and-true pitching stat you've seen on every baseball broadcast or box score from the past century, but it's very different. To start, DRA takes an event-by-event look at what the pitchers does, and adjusts the value of that event based on different environmental factors like park, batter, catcher, umpire, base-out situation, run differential, inning, defense, home field advantage, pitcher role and temperature. That mixed model gives us a pitcher's expected contribution, similar to what we do for our DRC+ model for hitters and FRAA model for catchers. (Oh, and we also consider the pitcher's effect on basestealing and on balls getting past the catcher.)

It's important to note that DRA is set to the scale of runs allowed per nine innings (RA9) instead of ERA, which makes DRA's scale slightly higher than ERA's. The reason for this is because ERA tends to overrate three types of pitchers:

1. Pitchers who play in parks where scorers hand out more errors. Official scorers differ significantly in the frequency at which they assign errors to fielders.
2. Ground-ball pitchers, because a substantial proportion of errors occur on groundballs.
3. Pitchers who aren't very good. Better pitchers often allow fewer unearned runs than bad pitchers, because good pitchers tend to find ways to get out of jams.

Since the last time you picked up an edition of this book, we've also made a few minor changes to DRA to make it better. Recent research into "tunneling"—the act of throwing consecutive pitches that appear similar from a batter's point of view until after the swing decision point–data has given us a new contextual factor to account for in DRA: plate distance. This refers to the distance between successive pitches as they approach the plate, and while it has a smaller effect than factors like velocity or whiff rate, it still can help explain pitcher strikeout rate in our model.

New Pitching Metrics for 2020

We're including a few "new" pitching metrics in the book for the 2020 edition, though unlike last year, these numbers may be a little bit more familiar to those of you who have spent some time investigating baseball statistics.

Fastball Percentage

Our fastball percentage (FB%) statistic measures how frequently a pitcher throws a pitch classified as a "fastball," measured as a percentage of overall pitches thrown. We qualify three types of fastballs:

1. The traditional four-seam fastball;
2. The two-seam fastball or sinker;
3. "Hard cutters," which are pitches that have the movement profile of a cut fastball and are used as the pitcher's primary offering or in place of a more traditional fastball.

For example, a pitcher with a FB% of 67 throws any combination of these three pitches about two-thirds of the time.

Whiff Rate

Everybody loves a swing and a miss, and whiff rate (WHF) measures how frequently pitchers induce a swinging strike. To calculate WHF, we add up all the pitches thrown that ended with a swinging strike, then divide that number by a pitcher's total pitches thrown. Most often, high whiff rates correlate with high strikeout rates (and overall effective pitcher performance).

Called Strike Probability

Called Strike Probability (CSP) is a number that represents the likelihood that all of a pitcher's pitches will be called a strike while controlling for location, pitcher and batter handedness, umpire and count. Here's how it works: on each pitch, our model determines how many times (out of 100) that a similar pitch was called for a strike given those factors mentioned above, and when normalized for each batter's strike zone. Then we average the CSP for all pitches thrown by a pitcher in a season, and that gives us the yearly CSP percentage you see in the stats boxes.

As you might imagine, pitchers with a higher CSP are more likely to work in the zone, where pitchers with a lower CSP are likely locating their pitches outside the normal strike zone, for better or for worse.

Projections

Many of you aren't turning to this book just for a look at what a player has done, but for a look at what a player is going to do: the PECOTA projections. PECOTA, initially developed by Nate Silver (who has moved on to greater fame as a political analyst), consists of three parts:

1. Major-league equivalencies, which use minor-league statistics to project how a player will perform in the major leagues;
2. Baseline forecasts, which use weighted averages and regression to the mean to estimate a player's current true talent level; and
3. Aging curves, which uses the career paths of comparable players to estimate how a player's statistics are likely to change over time.

With all those important things covered, let's take a look at what's in the book this year.

Team Prospectus

Most of this book is composed of team chapters, with one for each of the 30 major-league franchises. On the first page of each chapter, you'll see a box that contains some of the key statistics for each team as well as a very inviting stadium diagram. (You can see an example of this for the Milwaukee Brewers on this very page!)

We start with the team name, their unadjusted 2019 win-loss record, and their divisional ranking. Beneath that are a host of other team statistics. **Pythag** presents an adjusted 2019 winning percentage, calculated by taking runs scored per game (**RS/G**) and runs allowed per game (**RA/G**) for the team, and running them through a version of Bill James' Pythagorean formula that was refined and improved by David Smyth and Brandon Heipp. (The formula is called "Pythagenpat," which is equally fun to type and to say.)

Next up is **DRC+**, described earlier, to indicate the overall hitting ability of the team either above or below league-average. Run prevention on the pitching side is covered by **DRA** (also mentioned earlier) and another metric: Fielding Independent Pitching (**FIP**), which calculates another ERA-like statistic based on strikeouts, walks, and home runs recorded. Defensive Efficiency Rating (**DER**) tells us the percentage of balls in play turned into outs for the team, and is a quick fielding shorthand that rounds out run prevention.

After that, we have several measures related to roster composition, as opposed to on-field performance. **B-Age** and **P-Age** tell us the average age of a team's batters and pitchers, respectively. **Salary** is the combined team payroll for all on-field players, and Doug Pappas' Marginal Dollars per Marginal Win (**M$/MW**) tells us how much money a team spent to earn production above replacement level.

Ending this batch of statistics is the number of disabled list days a team had over the season (**IL Days**) and the amount of salary paid to players on the disabled list (**$ on IL**); this final number is expressed as a percentage of total payroll.

Next to each of these stats, we've listed each team's MLB rank in that category from first to 30th. In this, first always indicates a positive outcome and 30th a negative outcome, except in the case of salary—first is highest.

After the franchise statistics, we share a few items about the team's home ballpark. There's the aforementioned diagram of the park's dimensions (including distances to the outfield wall), a graphic showing the height of the wall from the left-field pole to the right-field pole, and a table showing three-year park factors for the stadium. The park factors are displayed as indexes where 100 is average, 110 means that the park inflates the statistic in question by 10 percent, and 90 means that the park deflates the statistic in question by 10 percent.

On the second page of each team chapter, you'll find three graphs. The first is the **2019 Hit List Ranking**. This shows our Hit List Rank for the team on each day of the 2019 season and is intended to give you a picture of the ups and downs of the team's season. Hit List Rank measures overall team performance and drives the Hit List Power Rankings at the baseballprospectus.com website.

The second graph is **Committed Payroll** and helps you see how the team's payroll has compared to the MLB and divisional average payrolls over time. Payroll figures are current as of January 1, 2020; with so many free agents still unsigned as of this writing, the final 2020 figure will likely be significantly different for many teams. (In the meantime, you can always find the most current data at Baseball Prospectus' Cot's Baseball Contracts page.)

The third graph is **Farm System Ranking** and displays how the Baseball Prospectus prospect team has ranked the organization's farm system since 2007.

After the graphs, we have a **Personnel** section that lists many of the important decision-makers and upper-level field and operations staff members for the franchise, as well as any former Baseball Prospectus staff members who are currently part of the organization. (In very rare circumstances, someone might be on both lists!)

Juan Soto LF

Born: 10/25/98 Age: 21 Bats: L Throws: L
Height: 6'1" Weight: 185 Origin: International Free Agent, 2015

YEAR	TEAM	LVL	AGE	PA	R	2B	3B	HR	RBI	BB	K	SB	CS	AVG/OBP/SLG
2017	NAT	RK	18	27	3	1	1	0	4	2	1	0	0	.320/.370/.440
2017	HAG	A	18	96	15	5	0	3	14	10	8	1	2	.360/.427/.523
2018	HAG	A	19	74	12	5	3	5	24	14	13	2	0	.373/.486/.814
2018	POT	A+	19	73	17	3	1	7	18	11	8	0	1	.371/.466/.790
2018	HAR	AA	19	35	4	2	0	2	10	4	7	1	0	.323/.400/.581
2018	WAS	MLB	19	494	77	25	1	22	70	79	99	5	2	.292/.406/.517
2019	WAS	MLB	20	659	110	32	5	34	110	108	132	12	1	.282/.401/.548
2020	WAS	MLB	21	630	92	30	3	35	102	85	123	5	2	.284/.382/.543

Comparables: Ronald Acuña Jr., Mike Trout, Tony Conigliaro

YEAR	TEAM	LVL	AGE	PA	DRC+	VORP	BABIP	BRR	FRAA	WARP
2017	NAT	RK	18	27	135	1.5	.333	0.0	RF(9): -1.1	0.0
2017	HAG	A	18	96	181	8.0	.373	1.0	RF(19): -1.9, LF(2): -0.3	0.9
2018	HAG	A	19	74	222	14.5	.405	0.3	RF(14): 1.1, CF(2): 0.2	1.2
2018	POT	A+	19	73	260	15.4	.340	1.4	RF(14): 1.0, LF(1): 0.0	1.6
2018	HAR	AA	19	35	113	3.6	.364	0.0	LF(4): 0.6, RF(4): -0.5	0.1
2018	WAS	MLB	19	494	125	40.5	.338	-0.5	LF(114): 2.7	3.0
2019	WAS	MLB	20	659	136	49.0	.312	1.4	LF(150): -0.8	4.9
2020	WAS	MLB	21	630	133	43.6	.310	-0.1	LF 3	4.8

Position Players

After all that information and a thoughtful bylined essay covering each team, we present our player comments. These are also bylined, but due to frequent franchise shifts during the offseason, our bylines are more a rough guide than a perfect accounting of who wrote what.

Each player is listed with the major-league team that employed him as of early January 2020. If a player changed teams after that point via free agency, trade, or any other method, you'll be able to find them in the chapter for their previous squad.

As an example, take a look at the player comment for Nationals outfielder Juan Soto: the stat block that accompanies his written comment is at the top of this page. First we cover biographical information (age is as of June 30, 2020) before moving onto the stats themselves. Our statistic columns include standard identifying information like **YEAR**, **TEAM**, **LVL** (level of affiliated play) and **AGE** before getting into the numbers. Next, we provide raw, untranslated numbers like you might find on the back of your dad's baseball cards: **PA** (plate appearances), **R** (runs), **2B** (doubles), **3B** (triples), **HR** (home runs), **RBI** (runs batted in), **BB** (walks), **K** (strikeouts), **SB** (stolen bases) and **CS** (caught stealing).

Next, we have unadjusted "slash" statistics: **AVG** (batting average), **OBP** (on-base percentage) and **SLG** (slugging percentage). Following the slash line is **DRC+** (Deserved Runs Created Plus), which we described earlier as total offensive expected contribution compared to the league average.

One of our oldest active metrics, **VORP** (Value Over Replacement Player), considers offensive production, position and plate appearances. In essence, it is the number of runs contributed beyond what a replacement-level player at the same position would contribute if given the same percentage of team plate appearances. VORP does not consider the quality of a player's defense.

BABIP (batting average on balls in play) tells us how often a ball in play fell for a hit, and can help us identify whether a batter may have been lucky or not...but note that high BABIPs also tend to follow the great hitters of our time, as well as speedy singles hitters who put the ball on the ground.

The next item is **BRR** (Baserunning Runs), which covers all of a player's baserunning accomplishments including (but not limited to) swiped bags and failed attempts. Next is **FRAA** (Fielding Runs Above Average), which also includes the number of games previously played at each position noted in parentheses. Multi-position players have only their two most frequent positions listed here, but their total FRAA number reflects all positions played.

Our last column here is **WARP** (Wins Above Replacement Player). WARP estimates the total value of a player, which means for hitters it takes into account hitting runs above average (calculated using the DRC+ model), BRR and FRAA. Then, it makes an adjustment for positions played and gives the player a credit for plate appearances based upon the difference between "replacement level"—which is derived from the quality of players added to a team's roster after the start of the season–and the league average.

The final line just below the stats box is **PECOTA** data, which is discussed further in a following section.

Catchers

Catchers are a special breed, and thus they have earned their own separate box which displays some of the defensive metrics that we've built just for them. As an example, let's check out J.T. Realmuto.

The **YEAR** and **TEAM** columns match what you'd find in the other stat box. **P. COUNT** indicates the number of pitches thrown while the catcher was behind the plate, including swinging strikes, fouls and balls in play. **FRM RUNS** is the total run value the catcher provided (or cost) his team by influencing the umpire to call strikes where other catchers did not. **BLK RUNS** expresses the total run value above or below average for the catcher's ability to prevent wild pitches and passed balls. **THRW RUNS** is calculated using a similar model as the previous two statistics, and it measures a catcher's ability to throw out basestealers but also to dissuade them from testing his arm in the first place. It takes into account factors like the pitcher (including his delivery and pickoff move) and baserunner (who could be as fast as Billy Hamilton or as slow as Yonder Alonso). **TOT RUNS** is the sum of all of the previous three statistics.

Justin Verlander   RHP

Born: 02/20/83   Age: 37   Bats: R   Throws: R
Height: 6'5"   Weight: 225   Origin: Round 1, 2004 Draft (#2 overall)

YEAR	TEAM	LVL	AGE	W	L	SV	G	GS	IP	H	HR	BB/9	K/9	K	GB%	BABIP
2017	DET	MLB	34	10	8	0	28	28	172	153	23	3.5	9.2	176	34%	.283
2017	HOU	MLB	34	5	0	0	5	5	34	17	4	1.3	11.4	43	32%	.194
2018	HOU	MLB	35	16	9	0	34	34	214	156	28	1.6	12.2	290	31%	.272
2019	HOU	MLB	36	21	6	0	34	34	223	137	36	1.7	12.1	300	36%	.219
2020	HOU	MLB	37	15	6	0	29	29	184	138	28	2.3	12.1	248	35%	.274

Comparables: Zack Greinke, A.J. Burnett, Aníbal Sánchez

YEAR	TEAM	LVL	AGE	WHIP	ERA	DRA	WARP	MPH	FB%	WHF	CSP
2017	DET	MLB	34	1.28	3.82	4.03	3.0	97.7	58	11	47.8
2017	HOU	MLB	34	0.65	1.06	3.08	0.9	97.5	59.6	15.1	49.9
2018	HOU	MLB	35	0.90	2.52	2.33	7.3	97.5	61.2	16.2	51.6
2019	HOU	MLB	36	0.80	2.58	2.51	7.9	96.8	49.9	17.5	48.3
2020	HOU	MLB	37	1.01	2.75	2.95	5.3	95.8	54.6	15.1	48.2

Pitchers

Let's give our pitchers a turn, using 2019 AL Cy Young winner Justin Verlander as our example. Take a look at his stat block: the first line and the **YEAR**, **TEAM**, **LVL** and **AGE** columns are the same as in the position player example earlier.

Here too, we have a series of columns that display raw, unadjusted statistics compiled by the pitcher over the course of a season: **W** (wins), **L** (losses), **SV** (saves), **G** (games pitched), **GS** (games started), **IP** (innings pitched), **H** (hits allowed) and **HR** (home runs allowed). Next we have two statistics that are rates: **BB/9** (walks per nine innings) and **K/9** (strikeouts per nine innings), before returning to the unadjusted K (strikeouts).

Next up is **GB%** (ground ball percentage), which is the percentage of all batted balls that were hit on the ground, including both outs and hits. Remember, this is based on observational data and subject to human error, so please approach this with a healthy dose of skepticism.

BABIP (batting average on balls in play) is calculated using the same methodology as it is for position players, but it often tells us more about a pitcher than it does a hitter. With pitchers, a high BABIP is often due to poor defense or bad luck, and can often be an indicator of potential rebound, and a low BABIP may be cause to expect performance regression. (A typical league-average BABIP is close to .290-.300.)

The metrics **WHIP** (walks plus hits per inning pitched) and **ERA** (earned run average) are old standbys: WHIP measures walks and hits allowed on a per-inning basis, while ERA measures earned runs on a nine-inning basis. Neither of these stats are translated or adjusted.

DRA (Deserved Run Average) was described at length earlier, and measures how many runs the pitcher "deserved" to allow per nine innings. Please note that since we lack all the data points that would make for a "real" DRA for minor-league events, the DRA displayed for minor league partial-seasons is based off of different data. (That data is a modified version of our cFIP metric, which you can find more information about on our website.)

Just like with hitters, **WARP** (Wins Above Replacement Player) is a total value metric that puts pitchers of all stripes on the same scale as position players. We use DRA as the primary input for our calculation of WARP. You might notice that relief pitchers (due to their limited innings) may have a lower WARP than you were expecting or than you might see in other WARP-like metrics. WARP does not take leverage into account, just the actions a pitcher performs and the expected value of those actions…which ends up judging high-leverage relief pitchers differently than you might imagine given their prestige and market value.

MPH gives you the pitcher's 95th percentile velocity for the noted season, in order to give you an idea of what the *peak* fastball velocity a pitcher possesses. Since this comes from our pitch-tracking data, it is not publicly available for minor-league pitchers.

Finally, we display the three new pitching metrics we described earlier. **FB%** (fastball percentage) gives you the percentage of fastballs thrown out of all pitches. **WHF** (whiff rate) tells you the percentage of swinging strikes induced out of all pitches. **CSP** (called strike probability) expresses the likelihood of all pitches thrown to result in a called strike, after controlling for factors like handedness, umpire, pitch type, count and location.

PECOTA

All players have PECOTA projections for 2020, as well as a set of other numbers that describe the performance of comparable players according to PECOTA. All projections for 2020 are for the player at the date we went to press in early January and are projected into the league and park context as indicated by the team abbreviation. (Note that players at very low levels of the minors are too unpredictable to assess using these numbers.) All PECOTA projected statistics represent a player's projected major-league performance.

Below the projections are the player's three highest-scoring comparable players as determined by PECOTA. All comparables represent a snapshot of how the listed player was performing at the same age as the current player, so if a

23-year-old pitcher is compared to Bartolo Colón, he's actually being compared to a 23-year-old Colón, not the version that pitched for the Rangers in 2018, nor to Colón's career as a whole.

A few points about pitcher projections. First, we aren't yet projecting peak velocity, so that column will be blank in the PECOTA lines. Second, projecting DRA is trickier than evaluating past performance, because it is unclear how deserving each pitcher will be of his anticipated outcomes. However, we know that another DRA-related statistic–contextual FIP or cFIP-estimates future run scoring very well. So for PECOTA, the projected DRA figures you see are based on the past cFIPs generated by the pitcher and comparable players over time, along with the other factors described above.

Lineouts

In each chapter's Lineouts section, you'll find abbreviated text comments, as well as all the same information you'd find in our full player comments. The only difference is that we limit the stats boxes in this section to only including the 2019 information for each player.

Managers

After all those wonderful team chapters, we've got statistics for each big-league manager, all of whom are organized by alphabetical order. Here you'll find a block including an extraordinary amount of information collected from each manager's entire career. For more information on the acronyms and what they mean, please visit the Glossary at www.baseballprospectus.com.

There is one important metric that we'd like to call attention to, and you'll find it next to each manager's name: **wRM+** (weighted reliever management plus). Developed by Rob Arthur and Rian Watt, wRM+ investigates how good a manager is at using their best relievers during the moments of highest leverage, using both our proprietary DRA metric as well as Leverage Index. wRM+ is scaled to a league average of 100, and a wRM+ of 105 indicates that relievers were used approximately five percent "better" than average. On the other hand, a wRM+ of 95 would tell us the team used its relievers five percent "worse" than the average team.

While wRM+ does not have an extremely strong correlation with a manager, it is statistically significant; this means that a manager is not *entirely* responsible for a team's wRM+, but does have some effect on that number.

PECOTA Leaderboards

If you're familiar with PECOTA, then you'll have noticed that the projection system often appears bullish on players coming off a bad year and bearish on players coming off a good year. (This is because the system weights several previous seasons, not just the most recent one.) In addition, we publish the 50th

Tampa Bay Rays 2020

percentile projections for each player–which is smack in the middle of the range of projected production—which tends to mean PECOTA stat lines don't often have extreme results like 40 home runs or 250 strikeouts in a given season. In essence, PECOTA doesn't project very many extreme seasons.

At the end of the book, we've ranked the top players at each position based on their PECOTA projections. This might help you visualize just how a given player's projection compares to that of their peers, so that even if a dramatic stat line isn't projected, you can still imagine how they stack up against the rest of the league.

Part 1: Team Analysis

Tampa Bay Rays: Where Are You Going, Where Have You Been?

Scott Orgera and Matthew Trueblood

2019: What Went Right

Way back in March when PFP drills were still taking place on sun-baked fields across Arizona and Florida, several prognosticators picked the Rays to win a wild-card spot on the strength of an upgraded rotation and what appeared to be a formidable cadre of bullpen arms. In the end, it was that pitching that played the biggest role in securing the small-market club's first playoff berth since 2013. Tampa Bay's 4.15 staff DRA and 85 DRA- were second to 107-win Houston in the AL, and their 3.65 ERA trailed only the Dodgers major league-wide. In a homer-happy season where a record 6,776 bombs were hit, the Rays kept the juiced ball in the yard more than any other club, allowing a mere 181 dingers.

Leading the pack was Charlie Morton, who signed a two-year, $30 million pact in late December. The right-hander relied heavily on his sinker over nine seasons in the National League, a span during which he experienced middling success but was never anywhere near top-tier starter status, before arriving in Houston in 2017. As is their way, the Astros completely revamped the veteran hurler's repertoire. They encouraged Morton to take advantage of his impressive spin rate by throwing more curveballs, offsetting them with four-seamers high in the zone. He'd pitch to miss bats rather than to contact, a complete reversal of what he'd been doing his entire career.

Morton's success continued in 2019; among other superlatives, his 0.7 HR/9 was a major league-best for starters. Despite being the club's elder statesman, he was the only member of the staff who stayed healthy from wire to wire. To no one's surprise, he was tabbed to start the Wild Card Game in Oakland. He didn't disappoint, allowing just an unearned run over five effective frames en route to his fourth career postseason victory. He was called on again five days later in another do-or-die situation, matching up against Zack Greinke with the Rays down two-games-to-none in the ALDS. Morton stepped up yet again, earning the win behind five innings of one-run ball against his former club in which he fanned nine.

Acquired last year from Pittsburgh along with Austin Meadows and a player to be named later (righty Shane Baz) in the lopsided deadline day deal that shipped former ace Chris Archer to the Steel City, Tyler Glasnow came out of the gate strong, putting to rest the control issues that plagued his development in Pittsburgh. He held opponents to a .202 batting average in eight starts before hitting the shelf in mid-May with forearm issues. He missed almost four months, returning in September for a quartet of abbreviated outings over which his tantalizing four-seamer/curveball combo was on full display. He finished 6-1 with a 1.86 ERA.

The team that pioneered the opener again successfully deployed the tactic, using it 43 times (27-16 record) after being forced to rely on the unconventional strategy much more than they'd planned in spring training. While utilizing the opener certainly skewed the numbers, the relief corps as a whole still worked more innings (772) than any other bullpen in baseball, compiling over a hundred more frames than the closest postseason participant (the Brewers with 670 2/3 IP). The only other playoff team in the top 10 were the Yankees, with 664 2/3 relief innings, and they featured a group of high-octane (and high-profile) All-Stars. Rays relievers were up to the task, however, leading the majors in ERA (3.66) and strikeouts (825), ranking fourth with an opponents' batting average of .231. Houston skipper A.J. Hinch called the Tampa Bay unit, "probably the best bullpen in baseball."

The most dominant of the group was the surprising Emilio Pagán, a righty who both refined his cutter and cut back on soda and carbs over the winter. He didn't break camp with the club but was called up in mid-April and eventually assumed full-time closer duties when José Alvarado and Diego Castillo succumbed to injury. The 28-year-old ran with the unexpected opportunity, notching 20 saves including 14 of 16 from July 24 on.

Castillo and Chaz Roe bore their share of the heavy workload and performed admirably, helping to keep opponents at bay and contributing to the Rays' 23-16 record in one-run tilts. Southpaw Colin Poche became a key piece in August and September after struggling mightily in his first exposure to big-league hitters. Manager Kevin Cash showed unwavering confidence in his young left-hander and it paid off down the stretch: Poche held opponents to a .136 average over his final 25 outings, fanning 32 in 25 frames.

Even Ryne Stanek and Adam Kolarek were mostly reliable before a pair of deadline deals sent them off to the Senior Circuit. The former netted the Rays right-handers Nick Anderson and Trevor Richards from Florida's other franchise. It was part of a midseason overhaul that thrust Anderson and Poche into significant relief roles. Tampa Bay was 76-5 when leading after six and 81-4 after seven, a testament to how Cash's relievers handled late-inning situations. The best story out of the Rays' bullpen was that of well-traveled righty Oliver Drake, who played for an MLB-record five clubs in 2018 and then spent the offseason and early spring as a mainstay on the transaction wire. The former Naval Academy hurler with the unconventional delivery was summoned to the bigs in late May and finally found a stable home in his age-32 campaign, pitching to a 3.12 DRA and 0.98 WHIP in 56 innings, striking out 11.3 per nine. What really stood out were Drake's reverse splits: He held lefties to a .360 OPS with 33 strikeouts in 104 PAs, compared to an .865 OPS vs. RHB, a figure inflated by 17 walks in 115 PAs.

After losing catchers Michael Perez and Mike Zunino (sporting a paltry .667 OPS at the time) to injury over a three-day period and briefly trying to fill the void with Anthony Bemboom, Erik Kratz and Nick Ciuffo, Travis d'Arnaud became the go-to option behind the plate and quickly stabilized a situation that could have easily derailed his new club. Second baseman Brandon Lowe was the early favorite for Rookie of the Year before fouling a ball off his right leg on July 2 and suffering a shin injury that later gave way to a strained quad during a rehab assignment in late August, a development that caused Cash to publicly state that the scrappy 25-year-old was done for the season. Lowe had other plans, returning for the regular season's final week and even hitting a crucial game-tying homer against Boston the following day. Fellow infielder Yandy Díaz was also thought lost for the year with a hairline fracture in his left foot but made an unexpected comeback in Game 162 and clubbed two homers off red-hot Sean Manaea in the Wild Card Game.

Left fielder Tommy Pham tied a career high with 25 steals and finished with 2.0 BWARP. Pham added two postseason homers, one off of ageless ace Justin Verlander. Willy Adames was a force on both sides of the ball in his first full big-league campaign, good for 20 homers and 3.8 BWARP. He had spent time in the offseason working on his defense and baserunning alongside Indians star Francisco Lindor and three-time stolen base champ Dee Gordon. Adames homered twice in October, also connecting against Verlander. First baseman Ji-Man Choi became a cult hero around St. Petersburg, finishing the regular season with 19 homers and a 117 DRC+ in 127 games. Listed at six-foot-one and 250 pounds, the former Korean amateur homered off of Zack Greinke in ALDS Game 3 and somehow managed to walk seven times in 22 postseason PAs.

The Rays handled the schedule in a manner as even-keeled as their skipper, winning 48 games both at and away from Tropicana Field and its infamous catwalks. They held at least a share of a postseason spot for 167 of 186 days, including the entire month of September. After handily dismissing the A's in the Wild Card Game, the Rays certainly made things interesting against the big, bad Astros. They came this close to earning the Kingslayer title, winning three elimination games over a seven-day span and remaining within striking distance until the eighth inning of Game 5.

2019: What Went Wrong

Glasnow's late-season success didn't carry over into October; he was tagged with the losses in Games 1 and 5 of the ALDS. While d'Arnaud was a godsend, the catcher position was in disarray prior to his arrival. This created a void in the lineup but also required the pitching staff to adapt to several brand-new backstops early on, something teams prefer to iron out in March. As with most clubs, other notable injuries also had an effect. Although the Rays' fill-ins did an admirable job for the most part, not having Glasnow, Lowe, Díaz, Alvarado, reigning Cy Young Award winner Blake Snell, Joey Wendle and others for extended chunks of time undoubtedly cost them a few games.

The team's overall offense ranked near the middle of the pack in the American League: their 99 DRC+ was eighth in the league, and they tied for seventh with 769 runs scored. Their 217 homers were 11th in the AL and only ranked higher than St. Louis (210) among playoff teams.

Prospect Outlook

The Rays had one of the best systems in baseball coming into 2019, and while they received an injection from the farm here and there (the unrelated Lowes, Nate and Brandon, were both above-average hitters), it remains one of the deeper organizations in the game. It also features the top prospect in baseball, **Wander Franco**, who isn't as far away as your average 19-year-old in High-A (if there even is such a thing). On the downside, there was a slightly ponderous Jesús Sánchez trade, and a major setback for Brent Honeywell, but neither is enough to move Tampa out of the top five farm systems around.

Brendan McKay had a bumpy major league debut, but there were flashes of "mid-rotation stalwart" along the way. He's the most obvious 2020 "prospect" help, as the arms behind him in the system (**Shane Baz**, **Matthew Liberatore**) are a bit further away, although they also offer more upside. Second baseman **Vidal Brujan** and shortstop **Lucius Fox** had uneven years, but righties **Joe Ryan** and **Taj Bradley** put their names on the map. Overall the Rays system remains quite strong, if a bit shallower than the past two years, due to the normal ebb and flow of graduations and prospect volatility. —*Scott Orgera*

2020 Outlook

Their pitching plainly wasn't broken, so Tampa's front office didn't waste time over the winter fixing it. Virtually every pitcher of consequence is back, and even trading far-off lefty Matthew Liberatore to St. Louis, they have terrific prospect depth in the minors, too.

Depth is the watchword on the positional side, too. Several players who contributed in unexpected, positive ways in 2019 had to do so because the team's Opening Day lineup and bench were so thin. Determined to avoid the same problem cropping up in 2020, Erik Neander made the aforementioned trade with the Cardinals, giving up more value in the long run to add a pair of quality role players who can make an immediate impact: José Martínez, whose best position wasn't available to him until he was dealt to the American League, and Randy Arozarena, who profiles as an excellent fifth outfielder. He also signed Yoshi Tsutsugo, who will take the bigger side of a DH platoon with Martínez, as an import from Japan, trying to create power upside and raise the lineup's floor at the same time.

At first blush, it's harder to explain the trade that sent Pham and infield/pitching prospect Jake Cronenworth to San Diego in exchange for Hunter Renfroe and (better) infield prospect Xavier Edwards. Pham was an important cog at the top of the order for Tampa Bay in 2019, but because of the similarity in the shape of his and Meadows' production, there was a bit of redundancy there. Pham and Meadows also have something in common in the field: they're not very good there. Renfroe brings big, raw, right-handed power to a lineup that didn't have it, and is a huge defensive upgrade over Pham. He's also four years younger and two years further from free agency. Between that last fact and the prospect sizzle around Edwards, Neander's intentions come into clearer focus. The Rays are always looking to the future, even when their broader offseason plan is to build upon a championship-caliber team. —*Matthew Trueblood*

Performance Graphs

2019 Hit List Ranking

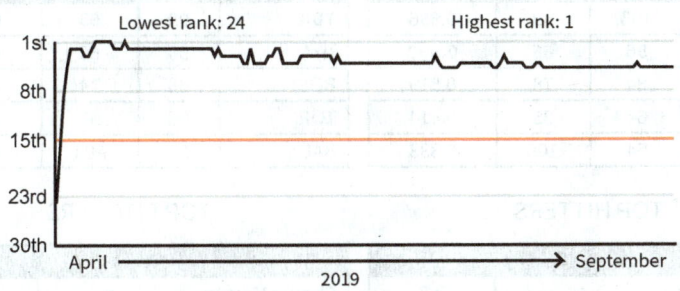

Committed Payroll (in millions)

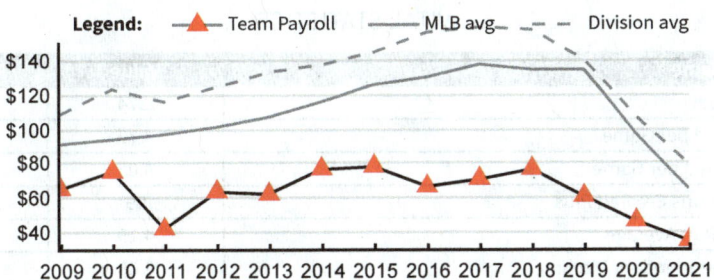

Farm System Ranking

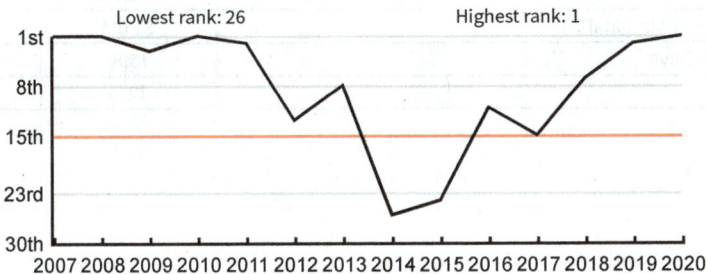

2019 Team Performance

ACTUAL STANDINGS

Team	W	L	Pct
NYA	103	59	0.636
TBA	**96**	**66**	**0.593**
BOS	84	78	0.519
TOR	67	95	0.414
BAL	54	108	0.333

THIRD-ORDER STANDINGS

Team	W	L	Pct
TBA	**99**	**63**	**0.613**
NYA	96	66	0.590
BOS	88	74	0.544
TOR	66	96	0.410
BAL	59	103	0.363

TOP HITTERS

Player	WARP
Willy Adames	3.8
Austin Meadows	3.7
Tommy Pham	2.0

TOP PITCHERS

Player	WARP
Charlie Morton	5.9
Blake Snell	2.5
Ryan Yarbrough	2.5

VITAL STATISTICS

Statistic Name	Value	Rank
Pythagenpat	.574	7th
Runs Scored per Game	4.75	15th
Runs Allowed per Game	4.05	3rd
Deserved Runs Created Plus	99	12th
Deserved Run Average	4.15	5th
Fielding Independent Pitching	3.68	1st
Defensive Efficiency Rating	.710	8th
Batter Age	27.2	4th
Pitcher Age	27.8	11th
Salary	$60.1M	30th
Marginal $ per Marginal Win	$1.0M	30th
Injured List Days	1396	23rd
$ on IL	12%	7th

2020 Team Projections

PROJECTED STANDINGS

Team	W	L	Pct	+/-
NYA	99.0	63.0	0.611	-4
TBA	**87.3**	**74.7**	**0.539**	**-9**
BOS	84.5	77.5	0.522	0
TOR	76.6	85.4	0.473	10
BAL	62.9	99.1	0.388	9

TOP PROJECTED HITTERS

Player	WARP
Mike Zunino	2.1
Willy Adames	2.1
Brandon Lowe	2.1

TOP PROJECTED PITCHERS

Player	WARP
Blake Snell	2.8
Charlie Morton	2.5
Yonny Chirinos	1.9

FARM SYSTEM REPORT

Top Prospect	Number of Top 101 Prospects
Wander Franco, #1	7

KEY DEDUCTIONS

Player	WARP
Travis d'Arnaud	2.0
Tommy Pham	1.9
Eric Sogard	1.5
Jesús Aguilar	1.2
Emilio Pagán	1.2
Avisaíl García	1.0
Guillermo Heredia	0.5
Austin Pruitt	0.4
Matt Duffy	0.2
José De León	0.1

KEY ADDITIONS

Player	WARP
Hunter Renfroe	1.6
José Martínez	0.9
Ronaldo Hernandez	0.5
Randy Arozarena	0.3
Manuel Margot	0.2
Kevin Padlo	0.1
Vidal Brujan	0.1
Lucius Fox	0.0
Brian O'Grady	0.0
Yoshitomo Tsutsugoh	0.0

Team Personnel

Senior Vice President, Baseball Operations/General Manager
Erik Neander

Vice President, Baseball Development
Peter Bendix

Manager
Kevin Cash

BP Alumni
Jason Cole

Tropicana Field Stats

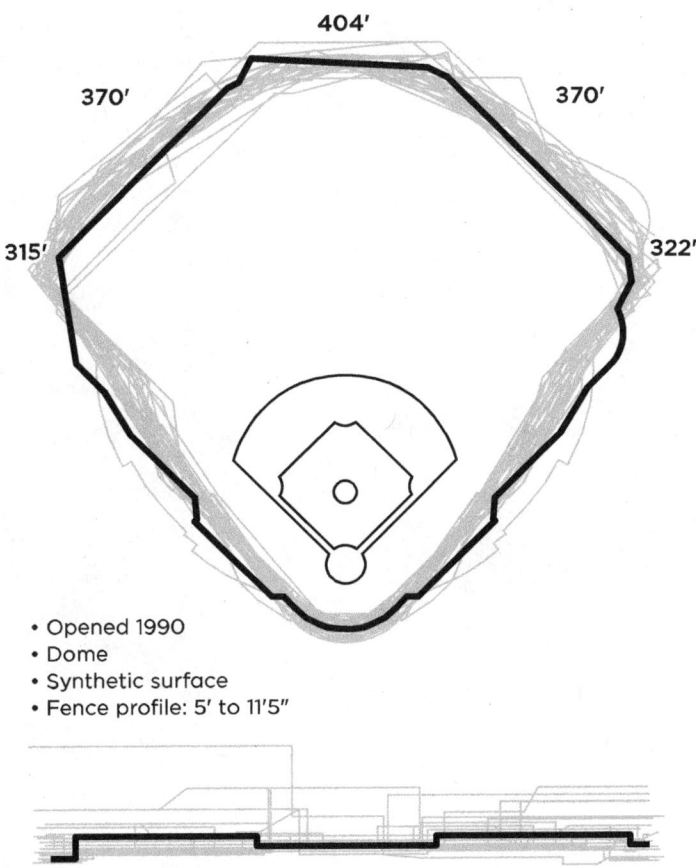

- Opened 1990
- Dome
- Synthetic surface
- Fence profile: 5' to 11'5"

Three-Year Park Factors

Runs	Runs/RH	Runs/LH	HR/RH	HR/LH
95	95	97	97	95

Tropicana Field Stats

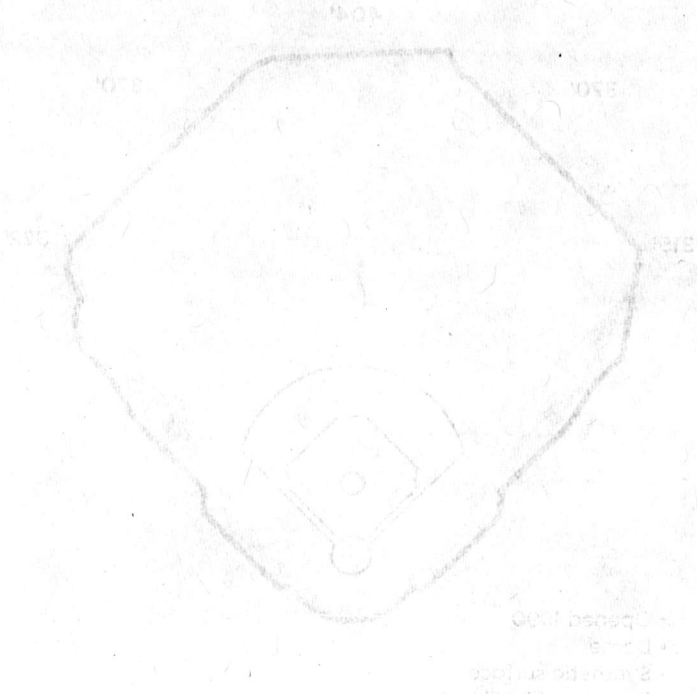

Three-Year Park Factors

Rays Team Analysis

"79. *I reviewed the conventional means of attaining the castle."*

If you were trying to describe the indescribable Rays in a sentence, you might come close with this: They're the Astros without money. Brainiac front office. Indifference to the bad optics of bad characters. (Maybe not the Astros' sign-stealing techniques.) Cy Young Award winners—each team has had two over the past eight seasons. During last year's offseason, Tampa Bay signed Houston's fourth starter, Charlie Morton, to a free-agent deal that made him the Rays' costliest player for about half of what the Astros paid Justin Verlander. Verlander won the 2019 Cy Young Award; Morton finished third. The reader knows quite well how the ALDS turned out, of course.

In 2019, Tampa Bay had no four-win position players (the Astros had two) and only two top-100 BWARP finishers (the Astros had seven). They had the best pitching in baseball even though their two stellar young starters, including 2018 Cy Young winner Blake Snell, spent much of the year injured and ineffective; they improved the staff at midseason by trading their favorite "opener," former first-round pick Ryne Stanek, for a reliever no one ever heard of, Nick Anderson, who did not rate even a Lineout comment in last year's *Annual*—and who was nearly unhittable as a Ray.

Off the field, Tampa Bay's front office proposed playing half their "home" games in Montreal, an eccentric idea quite in line with their unusual ways on it. The Rays break baseball into parts, seeking more than the sum—they led the league in relief innings pitched, unsurprisingly—and they operate from bases on opposite sides of boundaries. They aspire to the highest goal in sports, winning, with their sport's lowest payroll. They suffer from brutally poor attendance and are always trying to run away from home (they had MLB's second-best road record in 2019), yet over the years have built one of the game's strongest organizational cultures, not around a place or players or people but around a way of thinking. The departure to Boston of Chaim Bloom, the Rays' Senior Vice President of Baseball Operations (who cut his sabermetric teeth as a Baseball Prospectus author in the early 2000s), will probably change very little in practice, as Andrew Friedman's to Los Angeles didn't in 2014.

Yet that practice is remarkably adaptable. The franchise once known for homegrown talent has turned its approach inside out: by last season's end, nearly 70 percent of the roster originally came from outside the organization, a major-league high. Meanwhile, their 2013 fourth-round draftee, Kean Wong, was left to sandbag three full seasons and nearly 1,500 plate appearances in Triple-A, where he was an All-Star; he was finally called up in September 2019, got 14 big-league plate appearances, and was abruptly waived and claimed by another team. The Rays included Jesús Sánchez, the 32nd-best prospect in all of baseball, in the trade that brought Anderson from the Marlins. Just as Major League Baseball's franchises are now richer than ever, so too is its talent supply. (These are interdependent abundances.) There are more excellent players than any team can roster. The Rays know this, glean the field and thrive.

But how foolish it would be to continue on this way, writing conventionally about baseball's most unconventional franchise, applying practical craft to the work of prodigious theoreticians, and thinking organically where synthetics and bricolage obtain. Instead, the rest of this essay proceeds by compiling sentences from essays in last year's *Annual*, in adherence to the Rays' methods of breaking the game into parts and reappropriating other teams' assets. The assemblage includes at least one sentence from all but two of the essays in the 2019 Annual. Omitted are the essays about the Rays themselves, of course, and about Seattle because the Mariners are lately Tampa Bay's favorite trade partner and have been liberally acquired from already. The endnotes give authorship citations, along with other annotations where appropriate. Some sentences are fragments, breaking the game into parts. There are several ellipses, in the Rays' spirit of economy. Other sentences are taken out of context and placed in new ones in order to extract additional value; still others explore larger issues in the game and its business which the Rays' peculiar situation and approach exemplify or contradict, distort and critique. It is nearly impossible to consider the state of baseball without considering the Rays. Had they won the World Series, they'd have cleaved the very diamond as we've known it and forced front offices and fans to reexamine every facet.

Each sentence or string of sentences is given its own numbered paragraph. For background on this choice, the reader is referred to Donald Barthelme's short story, "The Glass Mountain," which provides the essay's epigraph.

⚾ ⚾ ⚾

1. How this team looks at any moment depends entirely on the light.[1]
2. The players are somewhere between incidental and academic. Mostly, of course, they are fungible.[2]
3. A sign that they had somehow transcended the usual pratfalls of modern baseball free agency signings.[3]

4. For a few weeks at the beginning of the season, they were a manifestation of the wildest dreams any baseball fan could have coming true.[4]
5. It's good to get to the party early in baseball.[5]
6. To leave the party early [...] in baseball, is far worse than arriving at the party too early.[6]
7. It's something of a cliché among wised-up sports fans that the worst place for a team to be is in the middle.[7]
8. The middle ground [...] is now considered baseball's Siberia.[8]
9. Winning without *really* winning.[9]
10. They became another team struggling with injury.[10,11]
11. No baseball team can fully protect itself against uncertainty.[12]
12. Trea Turner is just 25.[13,14]
13. In baseball, change is as inevitable as failure.[15]
14. In baseball, winning requires talent and strategy, but timing and luck cannot be discounted.[16]
15. (No one gets by without a little bit of luck in baseball).[17]
16. The best opportunity for certainty in baseball doesn't lie in a team's roster. It lies in a team's division.[18]
17. A team that looks fated to be stuck behind the same two teams in the division for the foreseeable future.[19]
18. In a world where sabermetric teams are always supposed to live for the future.[20]
19. The contention that had caught everyone by pleasant surprise.[21]
20. "Right up until it didn't work, it was great," Forst said.[22]
21. Maybe the 2015 Kansas City Royals are within dreaming distance.[23]
22. Baseball has experienced an influx of knowledge over the past 15 years.[24]
23. The waterfall of information pouring into every front office changes everything.[25]
24. It's no secret front offices, specifically analytical staffs, are more involved in the day-to-day operations than ever before.[26]
25. Some are hoping to improve without spending any money on improvements.[27]
26. You've all read *Moneyball*, right?[28]

27. We all read *Moneyball*, right?[29]
28. Did the "Moneyball" crew figure out some new market inefficiency?[30]
29. The A's took a page from Tampa Bay's handbook and started using an "opener."[31,32]
30. Lest we forget, what made Moneyball compelling as a sports narrative isn't that it's possible to build a cheaper, more efficient baseball team. What was compelling was seeing the possibility of winning from an apparent losing position through intelligence and cunning, and through finding what nobody else even thought to look for.[33]
31. In the past three years, the league's spending and competitive landscape has changed noticeably. The 2016 labor negotiations produced a joint bargaining agreement that, by nearly universal consensus, shifted power toward ownership. In the years since, teams have treated the luxury tax as a firm salary cap. Alongside, they have rushed to cut costs.[34]
32. Every owner ins baseball now has become an industrial strength scoundrel and acts as if the soft salary cap is a hard one.[35]
33. Because the owners have beaten the players as consistently in the court of public opinion as at the bargaining table, the partitions that separate business decisions from baseball decisions have all but disappeared. Teams have no problem whatsoever selling cynical financial choices to their fan bases as on-field choices merely focused on long-term competitiveness and analytics.[36]
34. Too many fans are willing to go along with it without any critical thinking.[37]
35. Contemporary baseball decision-makers have lured fans into the mindset that fuels amusement parks.[38]
36. There's usually an alternate source of entertainment.[39]
37. For [...] anyone who enjoys the game on the field more than the behind-the-scenes details of its production, they might be something of a bummer.[40]
38. The MLBPA has already started coming after clubs for failing to use their revenue-sharing checks for competitive purposes, namely the Rays, Marlins and Pirates. The Reds have only recently seen their payrolls reach similar lows to those culprits, and they don't have the history of cynical behavior the Rays and Marlins have exhibited.[41]

39. Incentivized cynicism.[42]
40. It's the media culture that perpetrates it.[43]
41. Cynicism at the top [...] shows up with unpredictable toxicity downstream.[44]
42. The chronic and usually well-compensated cynics.[45]
43. Welcome to Econ 101, with Professor Friedman.[46]
44. Welcome to MLB, a magical world where failure is success.[47]
45. Whether the counterintuitive process will be talked about as a major breakthrough within the game 15 years from now.[48]
46. In late 2012, MLB rounded out its national television rights package for a total of $4.2 billion through 2021, an average annual per-team payout of more than $40 million [...] In early 2018, every MLB team received a one-time payment of $50 million for the share of the stake in MLBAM that the league sold to Disney. In November 2018, Fox extended its national television rights deal with MLB for $5.1 billion through 2028, locking in a rate hike of more than 20 percent.[49,50]
47. A staggering amount of that value is entirely independent of the product the Reds put on the field.[51]
48. Oh, wait, and you have to play baseball?[52]
49. Many other streams of revenue therefore negating the loyalty completely.[53]
50. The watchwords of the modern MLB team are "financial flexibility."[54]
51. They've achieved financial flexibility.[55]
52. Financial flexibility is only valuable insofar as it's used to stretch for anything.[56]
53. Having key cogs making deflated pre-free agency salaries, including several near the league minimum, goes a long way in keeping a team's payroll below the competitive balance threshold.[57]
54. A clear victory for the model of efficiency that now has even competitive teams selling off mid-career stars.[58]
55. Major-league salaries exchanged for minor-league talent.[59]
56. The cost-cutting, the empty stadiums, the focus on acquiring those sweet bargain-value prospects even absent a cohesive plan to turn them into major-league ballplayers. It's all here and it's all frustrating.[60]

57. A system where talent is passively distributed [...] is the ideal system for baseball owners—especially the small-market cohort.[61]
58. The shame is that it shouldn't have to be.[62]
59. It's happening all over the league. But baseball fandom is provincial, so it's being felt only as it happens to each team, one by one.[63]
60. It's a situation we'll see many more times in many more cities before the trend stops.[64]
61. An endlessly repeating cycle that can seemingly never be broken.[65]
62. It's the economics of certainty.[66]
63. Baseball especially encourages its participants towards steadiness.[67]
64. To turn fleeting success into something lasting.[68]
65. We perhaps even began to take them a bit for granted.[69]
66. Pure joy should permeate what is, at its core, still a simple game.[70]
67. Does any of this matter?[71]
68. The question of baseball's purpose. It's far too messy and existential to unpack with any real satisfaction.[72]
69. The question now is: where are the fans going to come from?[73,74]
70. You can't just slap a new roof on a dingy, dilapidated dome and call it good.[75]

-Adam Sobsey is an author of Baseball Prospectus.

1. Jesse Spector, "Colorado Rockies."
2. David Roth, "Pittsburgh Pirates."
3. Russell Carleton, "St. Louis Cardinals."
4. Rachael McDaniel, "Los Angeles Angels of Anaheim."
5. Craig Calcaterra, "Atlanta Braves."
6. Ibid.
7. Roth.
8. Craig Brown, "Kansas City Royals."
9. Zach Crizer, "Detroit Tigers."
10. McDaniel.
11. The Rays lost the tenth most injury days in the majors, and the second most among playoff teams behind the Yankees, who set the all-time record.

12. Emma Baccellieri, "Cleveland Indians."

13. Meg Rowley, "Washington Nationals."

14. In December 2014, the Rays traded Wil Myers to the San Diego Padres in a multiplayer deal. One of the players they received was Trea Turner, whom they immediately flipped to Washington for Steven Souza, Jr., fulfilling a prior agreement. Souza played three seasons for the Rays. He was the team MVP in 2017, after which he was traded to Arizona. He missed most of 2018 and all of 2019 with injuries. By the time Turner turns 27 at the end of June, barring injury he will have played more games at shortstop for Washington than any player has for Tampa Bay in the history of the franchise.

15. Justin Klugh, "Philadelphia Phillies."

16. Nick Offerman, "Chicago Cubs."

17. Carleton, "Milwaukee Brewers."

18. Baccellieri.

19. Whitney McIntosh, "Toronto Blue Jays."

20. Carleton, "Milwaukee Brewers."

21. Klugh.

22. Susan Slusser, "Oakland Athletics."

23. Eric Nusbaum, "San Diego Padres."

24. Chris Cwik, "Texas Rangers."

25. Grant Brisbee, "San Francisco Giants."

26. Mike Axisa, "New York Yankees."

27. Roth.

28. Carleton, "Milwaukee Brewers."

29. Axisa.

30. Slusser.

31. Ibid.

32. Before the 2019 season, the Rays traded for Oakland castoff Emilio Pagán, who became Tampa Bay's most valuable reliever and de facto closer.

33. Jack Moore, "Cincinnati Reds."

34. Brendan Gawlowski, "Chicago White Sox."

35. Roger Cormier, "New York Mets."

36. Matthew Trueblood, "Arizona Diamondbacks."

37. Chad Finn, "Boston Red Sox."

38. Crizer.

39. McIntosh.

40. Trueblood.
41. Moore.
42. Robert O'Connell, "Houston Astros."
43. Finn.
44. Roth.
45. Finn.
46. Eric Stephen, "Los Angeles Dodgers."
47. Moore.
48. Cwik.
49. Trueblood.
50. In 2019, the Rays and Fox Sports regional network Sun Sports reportedly reached an agreement on a 15-year broadcasting rights extension worth $1.23 billion, or $82 million per season.
51. Moore.
52. Cwik.
53. McIntosh.
54. Jonathan Bernhardt, "Baltimore Orioles."
55. Baccellieri.
56. Ibid.
57. Stephen.
58. O'Connell.
59. Baccellieri.
60. Gawlowski.
61. Moore.
62. Spector.
63. Trueblood.
64. McIntosh.
65. Michael Clair, "Miami Marlins."
66. Brown.
67. O'Connell.
68. Ibid.
69. Offerman.
70. McIntosh.
71. Cormier.
72. Baccellieri.
73. Clair.

74. The Rays had the second-lowest attendance in the major leagues in 2019. They have finished last or second-to-last in every season since 2011, when they drew 18,879 fans per game. In 2019, they drew 14,552 fans per game.

75. Nick Nelson, "Minnesota Twins."

Part 2: Player Analysis

PLAYER COMMENTS WITH GRAPHS

Willy Adames   SS
Born: 09/02/95   Age: 24   Bats: R   Throws: R
Height: 6'0"   Weight: 205   Origin: International Free Agent, 2015

YEAR	TEAM	LVL	AGE	PA	R	2B	3B	HR	RBI	BB	K	SB	CS	AVG/OBP/SLG
2017	DUR	AAA	21	578	74	30	5	10	62	65	132	11	5	.277/.360/.415
2018	DUR	AAA	22	278	36	9	5	4	34	27	66	3	3	.286/.353/.412
2018	TBA	MLB	22	323	43	7	0	10	34	31	95	6	5	.278/.348/.406
2019	TBA	MLB	23	584	69	25	1	20	52	46	153	4	2	.254/.317/.418
2020	TBA	MLB	24	595	64	24	3	18	69	54	160	7	3	.242/.314/.400

Comparables: Milt Bolling, Jonathan Villar, Anthony Gose

If you are looking for an under-the-radar breakout candidate for the 2020 season, Adames is your guy. The sophomore struggled at the plate in the first half of the year, but after the All-Star Break he looked like a star in the making; his .278/.340/.467 line put him on par with players like Gleyber Torres and Amed Rosario down the stretch. Meanwhile, in the field, Adames had the highest FRAA among shortstops in 2019—a big step forward built on his range and an arm built for the left side. Still, at times those abilities get in his way. Of his 17 errors in 2019, 12 were on throws. Because he can get to balls most others may not, he tries to make every play even when the smart play is none at all. He's still rough around the edges, but Adames has all the makings of a dynamic two-way player that should hold down the six for the first half of the next decade.

YEAR	TEAM	LVL	AGE	PA	DRC+	VORP	BABIP	BRR	FRAA	WARP
2017	DUR	AAA	21	578	123	34.5	.354	1.1	SS(117): 0.1, 2B(11): 0.5	3.9
2018	DUR	AAA	22	278	110	15.0	.367	1.5	SS(62): 2.4	1.9
2018	TBA	MLB	22	323	100	15.7	.378	2.3	SS(75): -6.7, 2B(10): 1.7	1.2
2019	TBA	MLB	23	584	94	23.4	.320	2.9	SS(152): 12.2	3.8
2020	TBA	MLB	24	595	90	17.5	.311	3.0	SS 5	2.3

Willy Adames, continued

Batted Ball Distribution

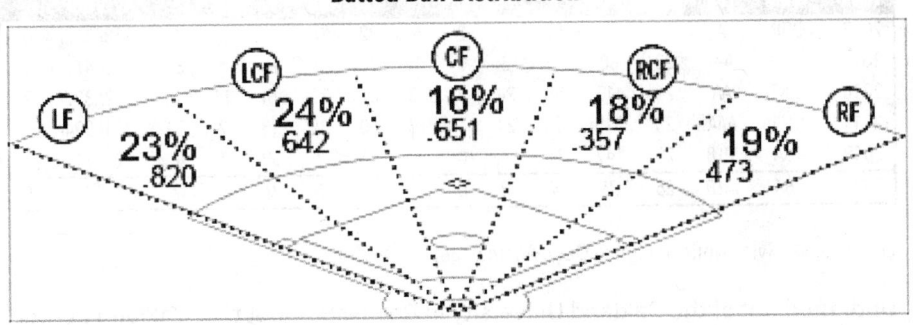

Strike Zone vs LHP   **Strike Zone vs RHP**

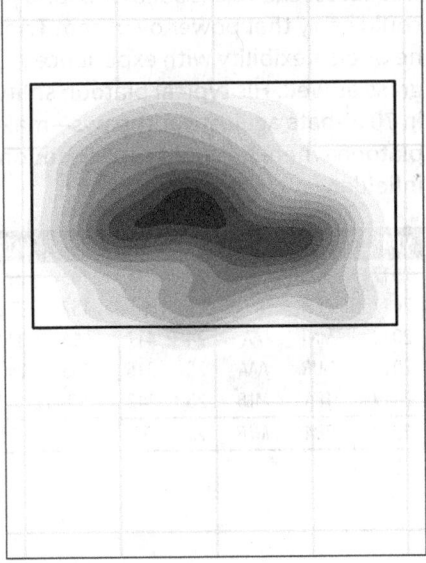

Michael Brosseau INF

Born: 03/15/94   Age: 26   Bats: R   Throws: R
Height: 5'10"   Weight: 215   Origin: Undrafted Free Agent, 2016

YEAR	TEAM	LVL	AGE	PA	R	2B	3B	HR	RBI	BB	K	SB	CS	AVG/OBP/SLG
2017	BGR	A	23	344	50	21	2	6	32	26	48	5	7	.318/.393/.460
2017	PCH	A+	23	80	13	3	0	1	10	5	15	4	3	.333/.425/.420
2018	MNT	AA	24	417	53	24	3	13	61	29	74	11	4	.262/.327/.449
2019	DUR	AAA	25	315	53	21	1	16	60	34	58	2	3	.304/.394/.567
2019	TBA	MLB	25	142	17	7	0	6	16	7	39	1	0	.273/.319/.462
2020	TBA	MLB	26	35	4	2	0	1	4	2	9	0	0	.243/.311/.425

Comparables: Tyler White, Rougned Odor, Adam Engel

Undrafted out of the Oakland University in Rochester—not *that* Oakland or *that* Rochester either—Brosseau defied the odds and made his major-league debut in 2019. Despite the lack of draft status, the right-handed hitter has been productive at every level of the system and was able to contribute in the bigs as well. Brosseau packs solid pop for a player his size and demonstrated that he could carry that power over from Triple-A without missing a beat. Defensively, he offers flexibility with experience at all three bases and has played on the grass as well. His typical platoon splits—hitting .300/.329/.500 with four homers in 70 at-bats against southpaws—make him well-suited to be the short side of a platoon where he could spell Brandon Lowe or another left-handed hitting infielder.

YEAR	TEAM	LVL	AGE	PA	DRC+	VORP	BABIP	BRR	FRAA	WARP
2017	BGR	A	23	344	145	29.3	.361	2.6	3B(31): 4.8, 2B(30): 0.0	3.4
2017	PCH	A+	23	80	157	5.2	.415	-2.2	3B(7): -0.3, 1B(3): 0.3	0.3
2018	MNT	AA	24	417	116	31.8	.290	1.4	3B(64): 3.7, 2B(16): 0.0	2.5
2019	DUR	AAA	25	315	135	24.8	.332	0.9	3B(32): -1.3, 1B(17): -1.1	2.0
2019	TBA	MLB	25	142	93	3.7	.345	1.0	2B(26): -0.5, 3B(18): -0.6	0.3
2020	TBA	MLB	26	35	96	0.6	.293	-0.1	3B 0	0.1

Michael Brosseau, continued

Batted Ball Distribution

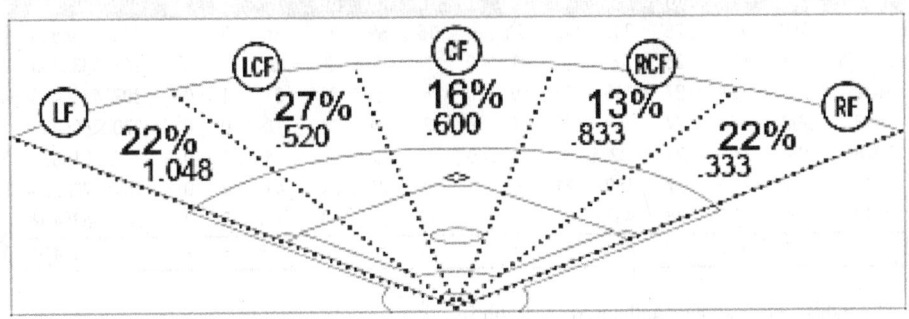

Strike Zone vs LHP   **Strike Zone vs RHP**

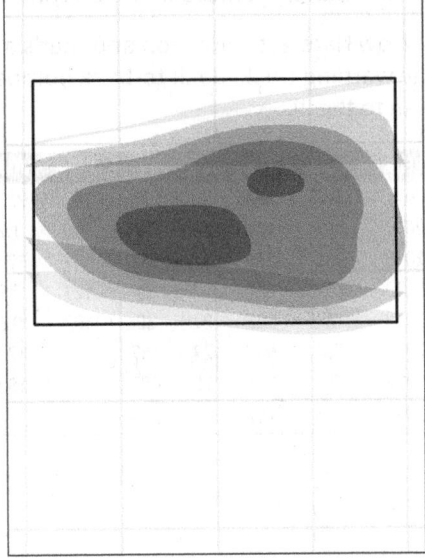

Ji-Man Choi 1B

Born: 05/19/91   Age: 29   Bats: L   Throws: R
Height: 6'1"   Weight: 250   Origin: International Free Agent, 2009

YEAR	TEAM	LVL	AGE	PA	R	2B	3B	HR	RBI	BB	K	SB	CS	AVG/OBP/SLG
2017	SWB	AAA	26	338	42	25	1	15	69	39	86	3	1	.288/.373/.538
2017	NYA	MLB	26	18	2	1	0	2	5	2	5	0	0	.267/.333/.733
2018	CSP	AAA	27	163	17	9	0	5	23	32	31	1	0	.302/.436/.488
2018	DUR	AAA	27	86	9	4	0	2	14	11	18	0	0	.270/.360/.405
2018	MIL	MLB	27	32	4	2	0	2	5	2	14	0	0	.233/.281/.500
2018	TBA	MLB	27	189	21	12	1	8	27	24	41	2	0	.269/.370/.506
2019	TBA	MLB	28	487	54	20	2	19	63	64	108	2	3	.261/.363/.459
2020	TBA	MLB	29	525	66	25	1	22	70	66	125	5	2	.247/.348/.450

Comparables: Bob Hamelin, Anthony Rizzo, Justin Smoak

They got options on my contract. I think they're sending me down. I can't believe this is happening in my own town. If I had wings I would fly, let me contemplate. I glanced in the box and I see my homie Nate (Lowe).

Now Nate got some pop and that's a known fact. We can both hit jacks 'bove the warning track. Back-to-back bombs cause it's on. N-A-T-E and me, the Choi-Man to the Ji.

YEAR	TEAM	LVL	AGE	PA	DRC+	VORP	BABIP	BRR	FRAA	WARP
2017	SWB	AAA	26	338	142	22.3	.351	1.7	1B(57): 4.3	2.4
2017	NYA	MLB	26	18	100	1.2	.222	-0.3	1B(6): 0.2	0.0
2018	CSP	AAA	27	163	139	12.3	.358	0.2	1B(38): -2.0, LF(1): 0.1	0.8
2018	DUR	AAA	27	86	121	2.9	.327	-0.9	1B(18): 0.2, LF(2): 0.0	0.2
2018	MIL	MLB	27	32	103	0.6	.357	0.3	1B(2): 0.0, LF(1): 0.0	0.1
2018	TBA	MLB	27	189	110	12.6	.310	1.9	1B(1): 0.0	0.7
2019	TBA	MLB	28	487	117	18.5	.303	-2.6	1B(103): -4.4	1.1
2020	TBA	MLB	29	525	115	18.5	.295	-0.3	1B 0	1.9

Ji-Man Choi, continued

Batted Ball Distribution

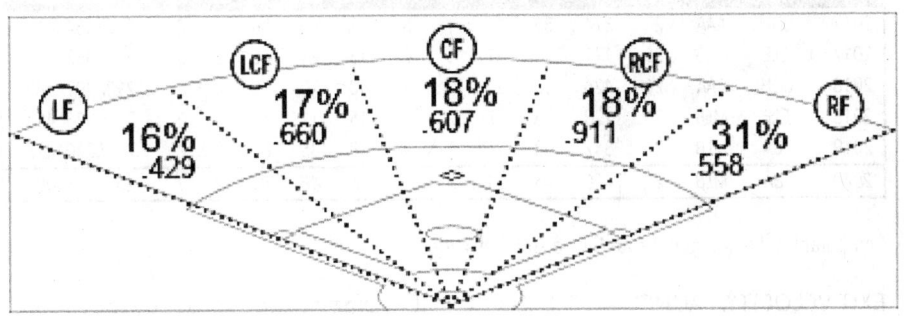

Strike Zone vs LHP   Strike Zone vs RHP

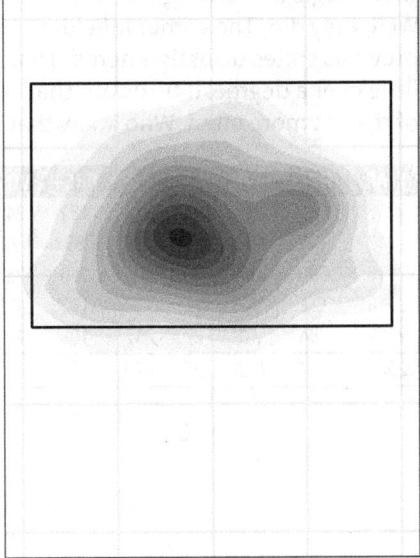

Yandy Díaz 3B

Born: 08/08/91 Age: 28 Bats: R Throws: R
Height: 6'2" Weight: 215 Origin: International Free Agent, 2013

YEAR	TEAM	LVL	AGE	PA	R	2B	3B	HR	RBI	BB	K	SB	CS	AVG/OBP/SLG
2017	COH	AAA	25	374	56	17	1	5	33	60	56	1	2	.350/.454/.460
2017	CLE	MLB	25	179	25	8	1	0	13	21	35	2	0	.263/.352/.327
2018	COH	AAA	26	426	53	24	0	3	40	70	75	2	3	.293/.409/.388
2018	CLE	MLB	26	120	15	5	2	1	15	11	19	0	0	.312/.375/.422
2019	TBA	MLB	27	347	53	20	1	14	38	35	61	2	2	.267/.340/.476
2020	TBA	MLB	28	420	46	21	2	10	46	48	80	2	1	.259/.346/.408

Comparables: Ed Sprague, Trevor Crowe, Rob Refsnyder

EXIT VELOCITY. LAUNCH ANGLE. OK BOOMER. Díaz was the go-to guy for various buzz words in 2019. Although he looked very much like a slugger with bulging biceps and had good exit velocity, Díaz entered 2019 with one career home run in 299 plate appearances. The narrative that would follow is the Rays sprinkled their magic launch-angle dust on Díaz's hulking arms and the home runs came. Well, they did. The corner infielder slugged .476, a mark higher than any of his previous stateside assignments. That said, his launch angle only increased by a little over a degree. It turns out that Díaz simply just hit the ball with the barrel of the bat more often. Who knew that would work just as well?

YEAR	TEAM	LVL	AGE	PA	DRC+	VORP	BABIP	BRR	FRAA	WARP
2017	COH	AAA	25	374	181	34.1	.412	1.1	3B(42): -3.4, LF(21): 0.7	3.9
2017	CLE	MLB	25	179	83	2.0	.336	-0.4	3B(40): -0.9, LF(3): -0.2	0.1
2018	COH	AAA	26	426	150	26.0	.360	-2.6	3B(73): -9.6, 1B(12): 0.2	2.1
2018	CLE	MLB	26	120	102	0.9	.371	-2.0	1B(9): 0.2, 3B(9): 0.2	0.1
2019	TBA	MLB	27	347	108	13.6	.288	-0.5	3B(50): -0.9, 1B(22): -0.1	1.2
2020	TBA	MLB	28	420	103	9.6	.305	-1.3	3B -3, 1B 0	0.7

Yandy Díaz, continued

Batted Ball Distribution

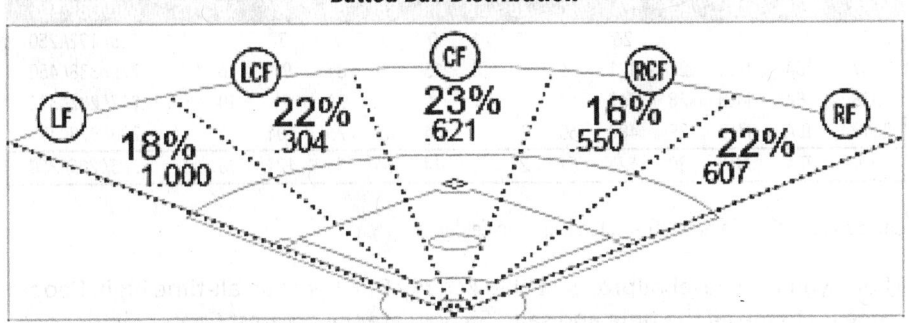

Strike Zone vs LHP

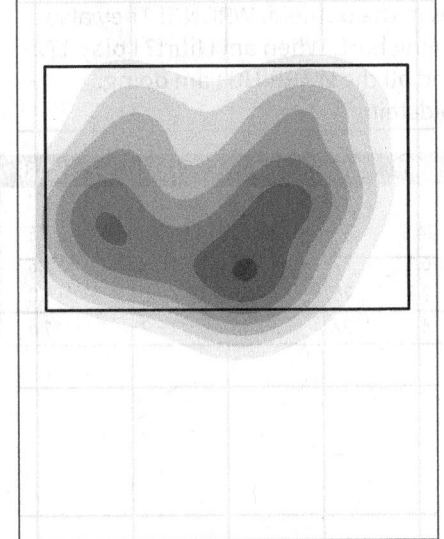

Strike Zone vs RHP

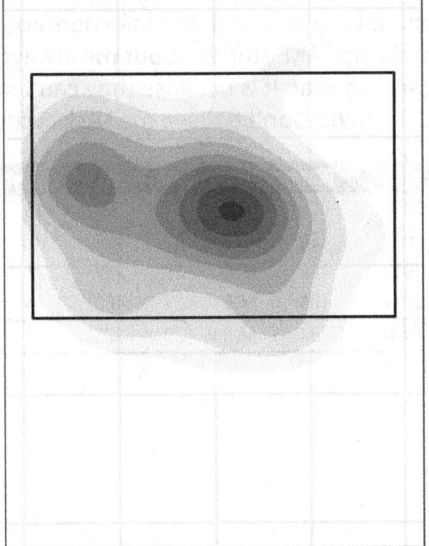

Kevin Kiermaier   CF

Born: 04/22/90   Age: 30   Bats: L   Throws: R
Height: 6'1"   Weight: 210   Origin: Round 31, 2010 Draft (#941 overall)

YEAR	TEAM	LVL	AGE	PA	R	2B	3B	HR	RBI	BB	K	SB	CS	AVG/OBP/SLG
2017	PCH	A+	27	26	2	1	1	0	1	2	7	0	1	.125/.192/.250
2017	TBA	MLB	27	421	56	15	3	15	39	31	99	16	7	.276/.338/.450
2018	TBA	MLB	28	367	44	12	9	7	29	25	91	10	5	.217/.282/.370
2019	TBA	MLB	29	480	60	20	7	14	55	26	104	19	5	.228/.278/.398
2020	TBA	MLB	30	525	51	21	6	14	56	35	121	16	5	.225/.285/.380

Comparables: Kole Calhoun, Glenallen Hill, Ivan Calderon

Thank you to @baseballpro. Just checked my DRC+ is at an all-time high. People come up to me all the time and say, "Sir, you are the greatest Center Fielder of All-Time." Maybe I am. Who knows. What I do know is I hit DINGERS and have a very high average. Very, very high average...some say the highest, but I don't know. I draw huge crowds at Tropicana Stadium even though the not-so-nice media lies and says my attendance is very low. NOT TRUE. Some even say that I am not a good hitter and take poor routes in the outfield. WRONG! They also make up FAKE stories about me always being hurt. When am I hurt? I play 172 games a year. It is because they can't stand all the WARPING I am doing. OUTLAW!!! Don't believe me? Ask @cdgoldstein.

YEAR	TEAM	LVL	AGE	PA	DRC+	VORP	BABIP	BRR	FRAA	WARP
2017	PCH	A+	27	26	15	-2.2	.176	0.3	CF(3): -0.3	-0.1
2017	TBA	MLB	27	421	101	24.5	.337	2.9	CF(97): 7.6	2.6
2018	TBA	MLB	28	367	76	6.1	.275	3.1	CF(88): 12.3	1.8
2019	TBA	MLB	29	480	75	2.2	.267	1.9	CF(125): 6.0	1.0
2020	TBA	MLB	30	525	77	6.7	.273	2.7	CF 9	1.6

Kevin Kiermaier, continued

Batted Ball Distribution

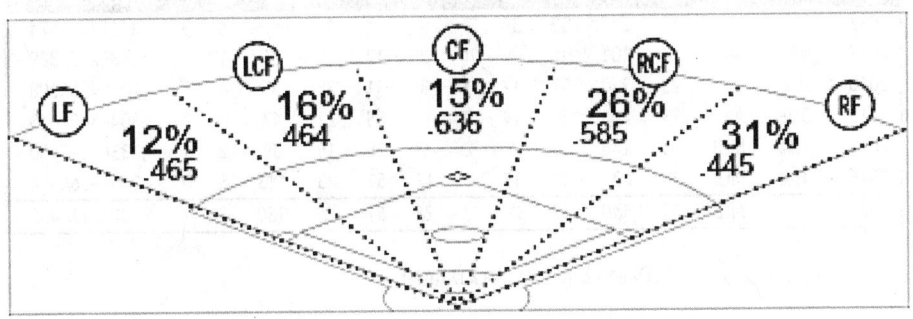

Strike Zone vs LHP   **Strike Zone vs RHP**

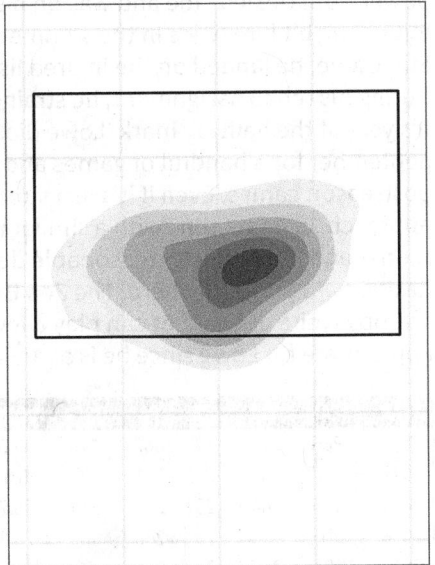

Brandon Lowe 2B

Born: 07/06/94 Age: 25 Bats: L Throws: R
Height: 5'10" Weight: 185 Origin: Round 3, 2015 Draft (#87 overall)

YEAR	TEAM	LVL	AGE	PA	R	2B	3B	HR	RBI	BB	K	SB	CS	AVG/OBP/SLG
2017	PCH	A+	22	367	62	34	3	9	46	47	65	6	3	.311/.403/.524
2017	MNT	AA	22	101	8	5	1	2	12	2	26	1	1	.253/.270/.389
2018	MNT	AA	23	240	37	17	1	8	41	35	55	8	2	.291/.400/.508
2018	DUR	AAA	23	205	36	14	0	14	35	22	47	0	1	.304/.380/.613
2018	TBA	MLB	23	148	16	6	2	6	25	16	38	2	1	.233/.324/.450
2019	TBA	MLB	24	327	42	17	2	17	51	25	113	5	0	.270/.336/.514
2020	TBA	MLB	25	560	69	24	2	28	81	45	180	3	2	.242/.311/.462

Comparables: Derek Dietrich, Danny Espinosa, Jack Dittmer

Not to be confused with the Lowe brothers—this Lowe rhymes with POW!—the second baseman received a six-year extension in the spring that should keep him in Tampa Bay's lineup for the foreseeable future. He has considerable power from the left side and was on his way to a 30-bomb season before the injury bug bit him twice in the summer. Soon after he was named to his first All-Star Game, he landed on the injured list after fouling a ball off his right leg. During his rehab assignment, he strained his left quad, which effectively ended his year at the halfway mark. Lowe did make it back to the lineup in late September for a handful of games and played in five of the team's six postseason games. Even if it's in a strong-side platoon role, Lowe should easily approach 30 home runs with a similar number of doubles. He's not a great runner and is a perfectly reasonable defender at the keystone with some flexibility to play elsewhere. The Zen Bobrist comp gets thrown around with scrappy white dudes that can play a few positions, but it seems more appropriate for Lowe since he is actually good at hitting baseballs.

YEAR	TEAM	LVL	AGE	PA	DRC+	VORP	BABIP	BRR	FRAA	WARP
2017	PCH	A+	22	367	178	39.6	.366	2.0	2B(75): -1.1, 3B(2): -0.2	3.6
2017	MNT	AA	22	101	70	0.5	.319	-1.3	2B(24): 0.8	0.0
2018	MNT	AA	23	240	161	25.7	.360	2.1	LF(26): 1.8, 2B(24): -3.2	2.2
2018	DUR	AAA	23	205	183	24.3	.339	0.4	2B(31): 1.2, LF(13): 0.9	2.5
2018	TBA	MLB	23	148	93	6.2	.279	0.8	2B(28): -0.6, LF(11): -0.3	0.3
2019	TBA	MLB	24	327	107	13.2	.377	2.4	2B(69): 3.3, 1B(5): -0.8	1.7
2020	TBA	MLB	25	560	104	24.9	.317	1.8	2B 0, LF 0	2.6

Brandon Lowe, continued

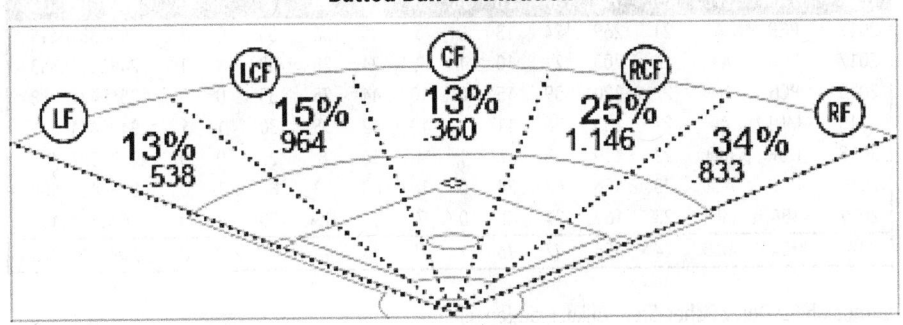

Batted Ball Distribution

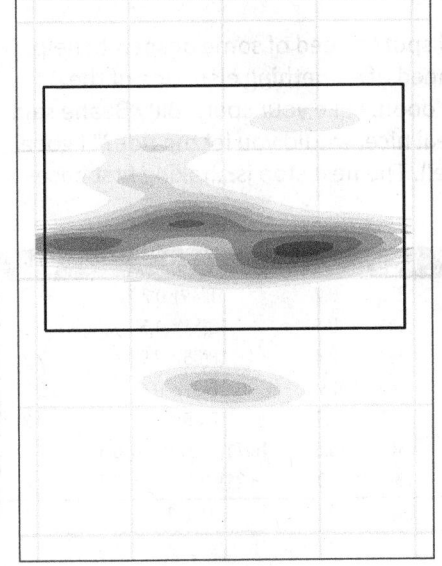

Strike Zone vs LHP

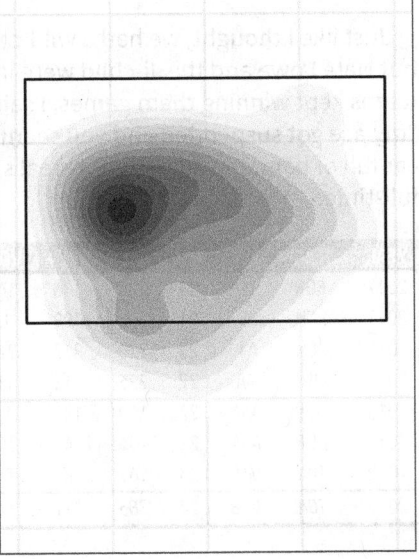

Strike Zone vs RHP

Tampa Bay Rays 2020

Nate Lowe 1B
Born: 07/07/95   Age: 24   Bats: L   Throws: R
Height: 6'4"   Weight: 245   Origin: Round 13, 2016 Draft (#390 overall)

YEAR	TEAM	LVL	AGE	PA	R	2B	3B	HR	RBI	BB	K	SB	CS	AVG/OBP/SLG
2017	BGR	A	21	269	34	13	0	5	35	36	53	0	1	.293/.387/.415
2017	PCH	A+	21	203	21	10	1	2	24	28	53	1	1	.249/.355/.353
2018	PCH	A+	22	220	39	15	0	10	44	25	33	0	0	.356/.432/.588
2018	MNT	AA	22	225	36	11	0	13	42	35	30	1	1	.340/.444/.606
2018	DUR	AAA	22	110	18	6	1	4	16	8	27	0	0	.260/.327/.460
2019	DUR	AAA	23	406	63	24	0	16	63	72	82	1	0	.289/.421/.508
2019	TBA	MLB	23	169	24	8	0	7	19	13	50	0	0	.263/.325/.454
2020	TBA	MLB	24	385	47	16	1	15	51	44	101	0	0	.252/.342/.440

Comparables: Derek Fisher, Steve Bilko, Brandon Allen

Choi is on deck and I'm in the hole, Nate Lowe is about to make some pitchers turn cold. Now they dropping and yelling it's a tad bit late Nate Lowe and Ji-Man had to regulate.

  Just like I thought, we had a wild card spot In need of some desperate help, but Nate Lowe and the Ji-child were in need of something else. One of the teams kept winning them games, I said "oooh, I like your spot." Billy Beane said "my ace got suspended and you seem real nice, would you let me ride?" I got a car full of banners and it's going real swell. The next stop is....taking first base full-time.

YEAR	TEAM	LVL	AGE	PA	DRC+	VORP	BABIP	BRR	FRAA	WARP
2017	BGR	A	21	269	136	14.1	.356	-0.2	1B(49): 0.2	1.3
2017	PCH	A+	21	203	109	1.0	.345	-0.5	1B(51): -1.5	0.2
2018	PCH	A+	22	220	217	22.6	.391	-2.4	1B(35): -2.9	2.2
2018	MNT	AA	22	225	218	33.7	.349	1.9	1B(39): -0.4	3.2
2018	DUR	AAA	22	110	121	1.4	.319	-1.2	1B(25): -0.1	0.2
2019	DUR	AAA	23	406	142	25.5	.341	-0.6	1B(71): -1.0, 3B(5): 0.3	2.3
2019	TBA	MLB	23	169	88	0.2	.340	1.0	1B(21): 0.1, 3B(4): -0.2	0.1
2020	TBA	MLB	24	385	111	11.6	.315	-0.6	1B 0	1.1

Nate Lowe, continued

Batted Ball Distribution

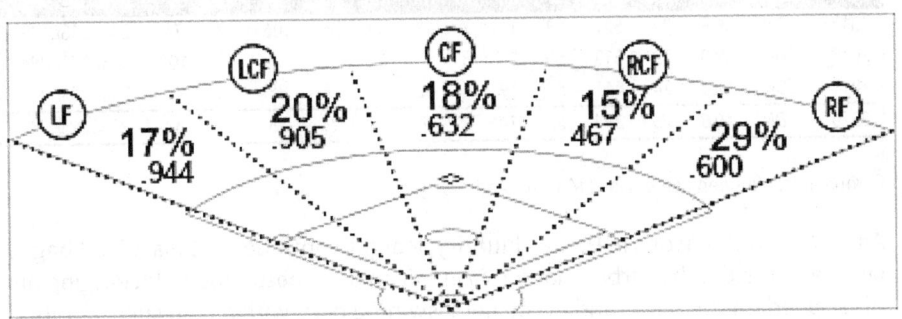

| **Strike Zone vs LHP** | **Strike Zone vs RHP** |

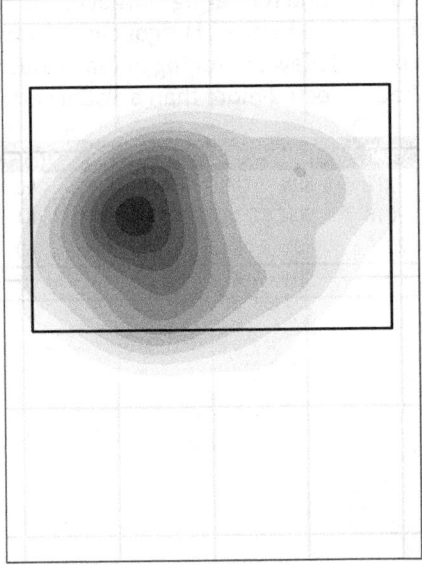

Manuel Margot CF

Born: 09/28/94   Age: 25   Bats: R   Throws: R
Height: 5'11"   Weight: 180   Origin: International Free Agent, 2011

YEAR	TEAM	LVL	AGE	PA	R	2B	3B	HR	RBI	BB	K	SB	CS	AVG/OBP/SLG
2017	SDN	MLB	22	529	53	18	7	13	39	35	106	17	7	.263/.313/.409
2018	SDN	MLB	23	519	50	26	8	8	51	32	88	11	10	.245/.292/.384
2019	SDN	MLB	24	441	59	19	3	12	37	38	88	20	4	.234/.304/.387
2020	SDN	MLB	25	294	28	14	2	7	30	21	58	10	4	.236/.295/.380

Comparables: Ruppert Jones, Lloyd Moseby, Andre Dawson

After three full seasons in Padres laundry, Margot continues to be a mixed bag. On the plus side, the turbo-charged Dominican did a better job of leveraging his plus speed on the bases and in the field, swiping bags with a high success rate and improving his jumps in center field. At the plate, he set a career high in home runs and lit up lefty pitching to the tune of .330/.420/.466. However, right-handers continued to work him over with all manner of fastballs, inducing weak contact and rendering Margot virtually unplayable against same-side pitching. Until that changes, Margot can capably man the short side of a platoon, pinch-run and play late-inning defense, but given his prospect pedigree, Padres fans had expected more than a SoCal version of Jake Marisnick.

YEAR	TEAM	LVL	AGE	PA	DRC+	VORP	BABIP	BRR	FRAA	WARP
2017	SDN	MLB	22	529	90	23.8	.309	1.3	CF(123): -1.0	1.2
2018	SDN	MLB	23	519	84	10.5	.281	0.9	CF(136): -4.9	0.4
2019	SDN	MLB	24	441	80	4.8	.272	4.5	CF(135): -4.6	0.5
2020	SDN	MLB	25	294	82	5.3	.278	1.1	CF -1	0.4

Manuel Margot, continued

Batted Ball Distribution

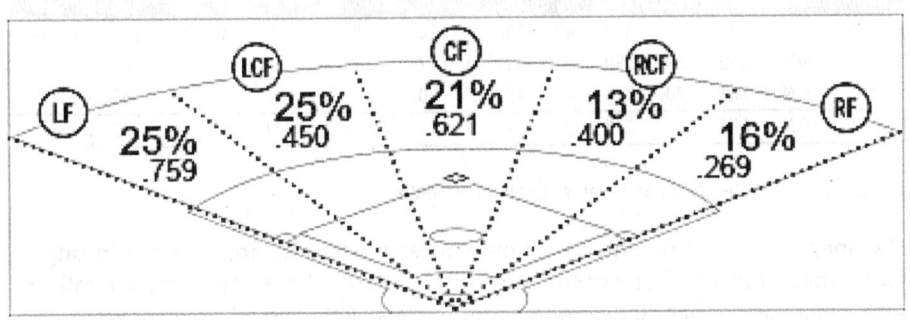

Strike Zone vs LHP   Strike Zone vs RHP

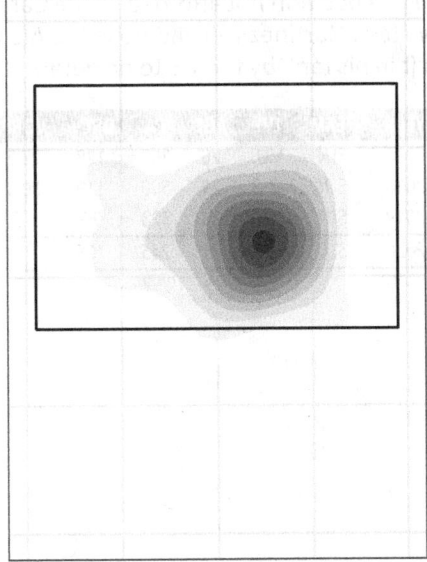

José Martínez RF

Born: 07/25/88 Age: 31 Bats: R Throws: R
Height: 6'6" Weight: 215 Origin: International Free Agent, 2006

YEAR	TEAM	LVL	AGE	PA	R	2B	3B	HR	RBI	BB	K	SB	CS	AVG/OBP/SLG
2017	SLN	MLB	28	307	47	13	1	14	46	32	60	4	0	.309/.379/.518
2018	SLN	MLB	29	590	64	30	0	17	83	49	104	0	3	.305/.364/.457
2019	SLN	MLB	30	373	45	13	2	10	42	35	82	3	0	.269/.340/.410
2020	SLN	MLB	31	245	27	11	1	7	29	23	51	2	1	.275/.345/.424

Comparables: Lee Stevens, Juan Lagares, Abraham Almonte

Martínez's immense height, Sideshow Bob-esque hairdo, and covered-in-bugs twitchiness make him one of the most distinctive-looking hitters in baseball. And, while his bat has slowed down, his contact skills and all-fields power enable him to remain an average or better hitter. Unfortunately, Martínez's baby-giraffe-learning-to-walk gait doesn't lend itself to glory in the field. His glove gives back most of the value his bat creates, leaving him best suited for DH—a position not afforded to the Cardinals or any other NL team. Eventually, we feel, Martínez will end up in the AL. When, where, how, and what he'll have left in his tank by then is to be determined.

YEAR	TEAM	LVL	AGE	PA	DRC+	VORP	BABIP	BRR	FRAA	WARP
2017	SLN	MLB	28	307	128	25.5	.350	0.1	1B(33): 0.0, LF(24): -2.8	1.4
2018	SLN	MLB	29	590	119	30.3	.351	-3.6	1B(84): -10.4, RF(46): 0.2	0.9
2019	SLN	MLB	30	373	94	6.2	.328	0.7	RF(75): -3.5, LF(7): 0.0	0.3
2020	SLN	MLB	31	245	108	8.3	.330	-0.4	RF -1, LF -1	0.6

José Martínez, continued

Batted Ball Distribution

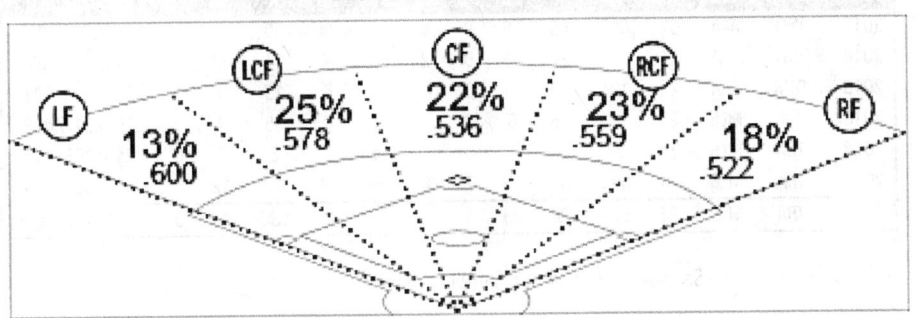

Strike Zone vs LHP   **Strike Zone vs RHP**

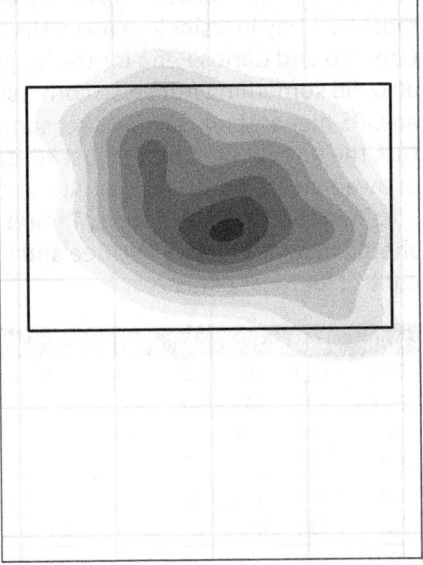

Austin Meadows RF

Born: 05/03/95   Age: 25   Bats: L   Throws: L
Height: 6'3"   Weight: 220   Origin: Round 1, 2013 Draft (#9 overall)

YEAR	TEAM	LVL	AGE	PA	R	2B	3B	HR	RBI	BB	K	SB	CS	AVG/OBP/SLG
2017	IND	AAA	22	312	48	19	0	4	36	24	50	11	3	.250/.311/.359
2018	IND	AAA	23	179	27	13	0	2	21	9	24	11	1	.279/.318/.394
2018	DUR	AAA	23	106	19	11	0	10	22	8	13	1	1	.344/.396/.771
2018	PIT	MLB	23	165	16	8	2	5	13	8	35	4	1	.292/.327/.468
2018	TBA	MLB	23	26	3	1	0	1	4	2	5	1	0	.250/.308/.417
2019	TBA	MLB	24	591	83	29	7	33	89	54	131	12	7	.291/.364/.558
2020	TBA	MLB	25	595	78	28	5	30	90	49	130	16	5	.272/.337/.507

Comparables: Michael Saunders, Clint Frazier, Cameron Maybin

Meadows' first full season in the big leagues went about as well as you could have hoped. He was the best player on a 96-win team and led the Rays in almost every offensive statistic. Meadows continued the power surge he showed late last season after his trade from Pittsburgh. His 33 home runs were the seventh most by a Ray in a single season. His .558 slugging percentage trailed just José Canseco and Carlos Peña for the highest team mark in a single year. Meadows also did something franchise cornerstone Evan Longoria was unable to do: post an OPS higher than .900 for a season. Considering his injury past and the home turf, the Rays limited him to just 86 starts in the field. The load management allowed him to play nearly a full season despite missing some time with a sprained thumb. In Meadows, Tampa Bay has an All-Star caliber hitter that should be worth between three and five wins a season and is under team control for most of his 20s.

YEAR	TEAM	LVL	AGE	PA	DRC+	VORP	BABIP	BRR	FRAA	WARP
2017	IND	AAA	22	312	92	9.0	.289	3.7	CF(33): -1.9, LF(24): -0.8	0.7
2018	IND	AAA	23	179	154	8.3	.314	2.4	CF(22): -1.5, LF(18): 0.1	2.1
2018	DUR	AAA	23	106	157	14.9	.311	-1.6	CF(17): -1.2, RF(4): -0.2	1.6
2018	PIT	MLB	23	165	95	8.1	.345	-1.1	CF(15): -0.7, RF(13): -1.1	0.1
2018	TBA	MLB	23	26	95	0.4	.278	-0.1	RF(7): -1.4, LF(1): 0.0	-0.1
2019	TBA	MLB	24	591	135	40.3	.331	-3.5	RF(57): -3.5, LF(34): 4.6	3.7
2020	TBA	MLB	25	595	122	30.0	.308	-2.3	RF-9, CF-1	2.1

Austin Meadows, continued

Batted Ball Distribution

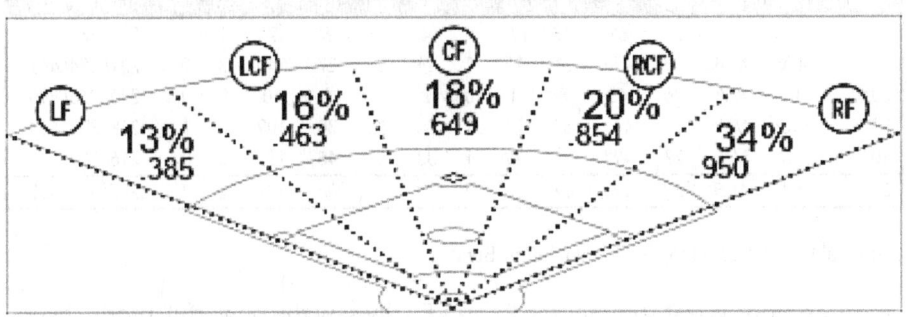

Strike Zone vs LHP   Strike Zone vs RHP

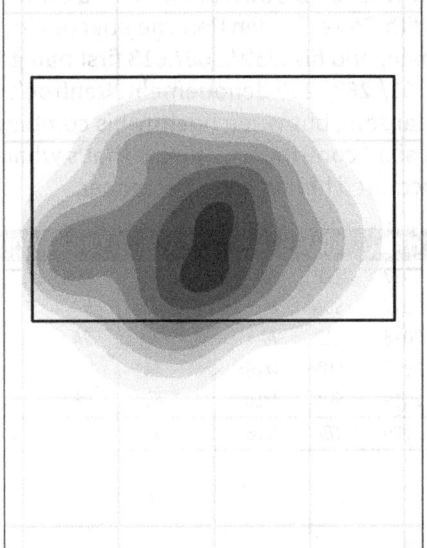

Rays Player Analysis - 45

Hunter Renfroe OF

Born: 01/28/92 Age: 28 Bats: R Throws: R
Height: 6'1" Weight: 220 Origin: Round 1, 2013 Draft (#13 overall)

YEAR	TEAM	LVL	AGE	PA	R	2B	3B	HR	RBI	BB	K	SB	CS	AVG/OBP/SLG
2017	ELP	AAA	25	61	18	7	1	4	18	6	7	1	0	.509/.557/.891
2017	SDN	MLB	25	479	51	25	1	26	58	27	140	3	0	.231/.284/.467
2018	ELP	AAA	26	43	6	1	0	2	4	2	10	0	0	.220/.256/.390
2018	SDN	MLB	26	441	53	23	1	26	68	30	109	2	1	.248/.302/.504
2019	SDN	MLB	27	494	64	19	1	33	64	46	154	5	0	.216/.289/.489
2020	TBA	MLB	28	490	67	26	2	33	84	36	147	2	1	.245/.306/.529

Comparables: Jose Canseco, Jay Buhner, Bobby Bonds

For three months last summer the Padres finally saw the powerful, productive right fielder they thought they had popped with their first pick in the 2013 draft. Renfroe was not only playing excellent outfield defense and denting baseballs on his way to the first 30-bomb season by a Padres outfielder this century, but he ratcheted down his whiff and on-base rates from "Insufferable" to "Sufferable With Power." Then Renfroe augered in, possibly due to nagging foot and ankle pain, and his .252/.308/.613 first half gave way to a punchless and contact-free .161/.263/.299 denouement. Renfroe's hacktastic ways will always prevent stardom, but when healthy his combination of power and leather can make him a solid contributor. At least that's what the Rays were thinking when they acquired him in early December.

YEAR	TEAM	LVL	AGE	PA	DRC+	VORP	BABIP	BRR	FRAA	WARP
2017	ELP	AAA	25	61	236	17.2	.545	0.8	RF(12): 1.9	1.4
2017	SDN	MLB	25	479	94	15.9	.275	-0.9	RF(120): -2.1	0.4
2018	ELP	AAA	26	43	74	-0.8	.241	-0.1	RF(9): 2.4	0.2
2018	SDN	MLB	26	441	110	18.9	.271	-1.2	LF(58): -1.3, RF(50): 6.6	2.0
2019	SDN	MLB	27	494	98	11.9	.239	-2.2	RF(86): 6.5, LF(67): 0.7	1.6
2020	TBA	MLB	28	490	114	20.2	.287	-1.5	LF 1, RF 1	2.4

Hunter Renfroe, continued

Batted Ball Distribution

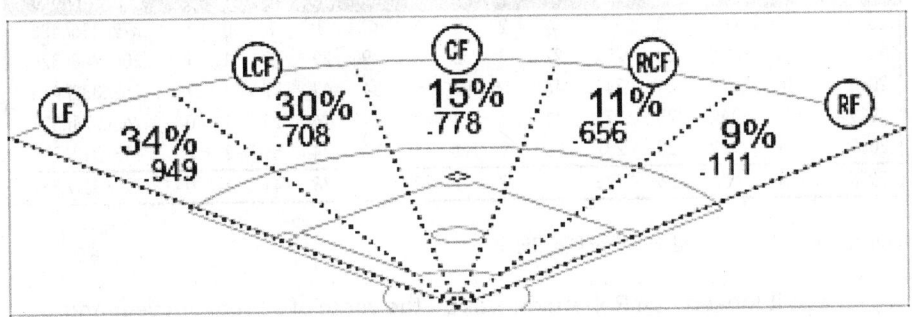

Strike Zone vs LHP

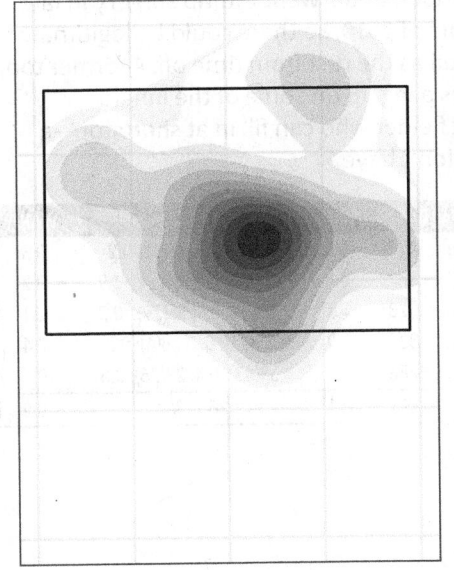

Strike Zone vs RHP

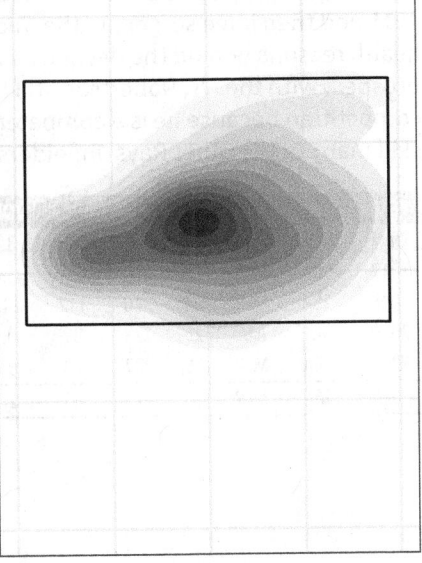

Daniel Robertson   UT

Born: 03/22/94   Age: 26   Bats: R   Throws: R
Height: 5'11"   Weight: 200   Origin: Round 1, 2012 Draft (#34 overall)

YEAR	TEAM	LVL	AGE	PA	R	2B	3B	HR	RBI	BB	K	SB	CS	AVG/OBP/SLG
2017	DUR	AAA	23	47	7	2	0	1	1	3	7	0	1	.372/.426/.488
2017	TBA	MLB	23	254	22	7	2	5	19	29	73	1	1	.206/.308/.326
2018	TBA	MLB	24	340	46	16	0	9	34	43	77	2	2	.262/.382/.415
2019	DUR	AAA	25	123	11	1	0	2	9	16	25	1	0	.260/.374/.327
2019	TBA	MLB	25	237	23	9	1	2	19	24	59	2	2	.213/.312/.295
2020	TBA	MLB	26	175	17	7	1	3	17	18	44	1	0	.227/.327/.349

Comparables: J.P. Crawford, Nick Franklin, Rio Ruiz

A year ago it looked as if Robertson was on the verge of a breakout year and earning an everyday role with the Rays. After an abysmal 2019, he is just looking to make the roster this spring. His discipline rates remained close enough to 2018 to offer some hope, but the biggest difference was a 50-point drop in BABIP and a huge drop in power output. Robertson underwent thumb surgery in late 2018 and then knee surgery in the middle of 2019, so there could be legitimate health reasons behind the decline as well as the rust from time off. A former top prospect with the A's, Robertson still has a leg up on some of the infield competition because he is a competent fielder who can fill in at shortstop—a skill many of the other Rays' infielders don't have.

YEAR	TEAM	LVL	AGE	PA	DRC+	VORP	BABIP	BRR	FRAA	WARP
2017	DUR	AAA	23	47	143	3.1	.429	-1.0	SS(4): 0.3, 3B(3): -0.2	0.3
2017	TBA	MLB	23	254	79	1.4	.282	-0.8	2B(41): -2.2, SS(24): 1.9	0.2
2018	TBA	MLB	24	340	112	24.7	.328	1.8	2B(39): 3.1, SS(29): -0.3	2.1
2019	DUR	AAA	25	123	89	0.4	.325	-0.7	SS(21): 0.7, 2B(4): 0.2	0.4
2019	TBA	MLB	25	237	73	0.8	.288	-1.4	3B(43): 0.4, 2B(26): 0.5	0.1
2020	TBA	MLB	26	175	85	2.6	.299	0.1	2B 1, 3B 0	0.5

Daniel Robertson, continued

Batted Ball Distribution

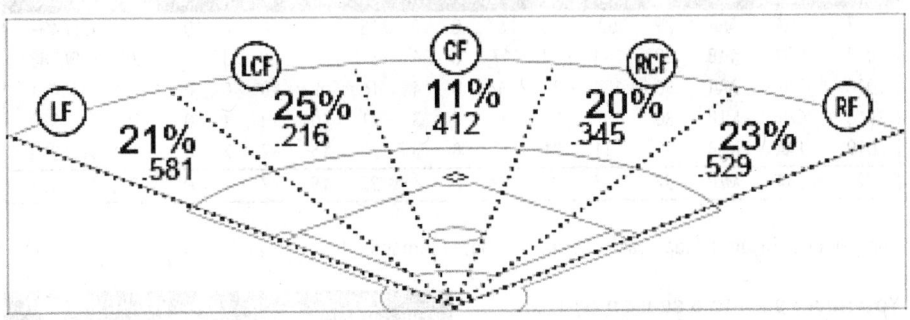

Strike Zone vs LHP **Strike Zone vs RHP**

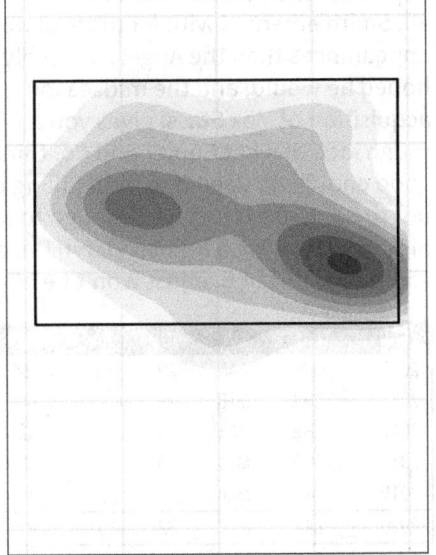

Tampa Bay Rays 2020

Kevan Smith   C
Born: 06/28/88   Age: 32   Bats: R   Throws: R
Height: 6'4"   Weight: 240   Origin: Round 7, 2011 Draft (#231 overall)

YEAR	TEAM	LVL	AGE	PA	R	2B	3B	HR	RBI	BB	K	SB	CS	AVG/OBP/SLG
2017	CHR	AAA	29	62	10	6	0	0	15	6	9	0	0	.377/.435/.491
2017	CHA	MLB	29	294	23	17	0	4	30	9	46	0	0	.283/.309/.388
2018	CHR	AAA	30	124	12	4	0	4	16	8	18	0	0	.268/.331/.411
2018	CHA	MLB	30	187	21	6	0	3	21	10	18	1	0	.292/.348/.380
2019	LAA	MLB	31	211	21	12	0	5	20	16	37	2	0	.251/.318/.393
2020	LAA	MLB	32	251	25	12	0	6	27	18	47	1	0	.246/.310/.381

Comparables: Bryan Holaday, Jason Jaramillo, Chase d'Arnaud

YEAR	TEAM	P. COUNT	FRM RUNS	BLK RUNS	THRW RUNS	TOT RUNS
2017	CHA	10862	1.6	-1.6	-3.9	-4.5
2017	CHR	1944	0.1	-0.4	-0.1	-0.4
2018	CHA	6961	1.5	-0.9	-0.3	0.7
2018	CHR	2973	0.4	-0.8	-0.2	-0.5
2019	LAA	7453	-4.3	-2.0	-0.7	-6.9
2020	LAA	9904	-2.5	-0.4	-1.0	-3.9

You never go into a season with a catcher like Smith as your Plan A. He backed up Omar Narváez in Chicago in 2018, and began 2019 backing up Jonathan Lucroy in Anaheim. Still and all, Smith emerged with far more plate appearances than the Angels probably hoped he would, and the midseason acquisition of Max Stassi gives you a rough idea of what Eppler and Co. think of the 31-year-old. The hitting is just good enough to keep him from falling entirely out of the picture in the present, but the defense is just bad enough to shorten his shelf life as a backup deep into his 30s. Following a non-tender in December, Smith will likely spend 2020 as somebody's Plan B, it just won't be in the Big A.

YEAR	TEAM	LVL	AGE	PA	DRC+	VORP	BABIP	BRR	FRAA	WARP
2017	CHR	AAA	29	62	164	5.4	.435	0.5	C(13): -0.2	0.7
2017	CHA	MLB	29	294	80	6.8	.323	0.5	C(79): -6.2	0.1
2018	CHR	AAA	30	124	102	2.6	.286	-1.0	C(22): -0.7	0.3
2018	CHA	MLB	30	187	101	7.2	.311	0.2	C(47): 0.1	1.0
2019	LAA	MLB	31	211	89	7.4	.287	-1.2		-0.2
2020	LAA	MLB	32	251	83	2.3	.285	-0.2	C -5	-0.2

Kevan Smith, continued

Batted Ball Distribution

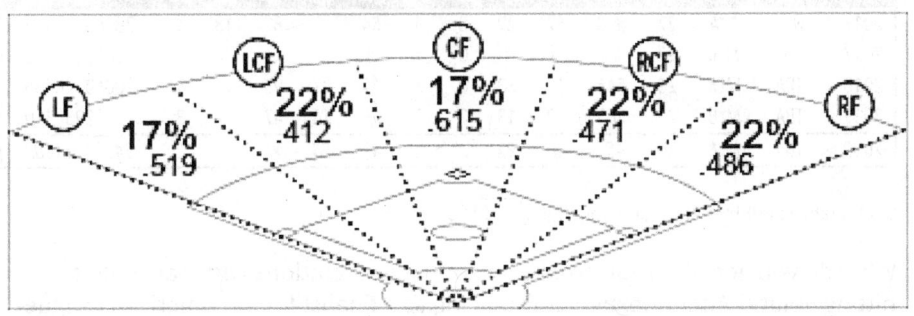

Strike Zone vs LHP   **Strike Zone vs RHP**

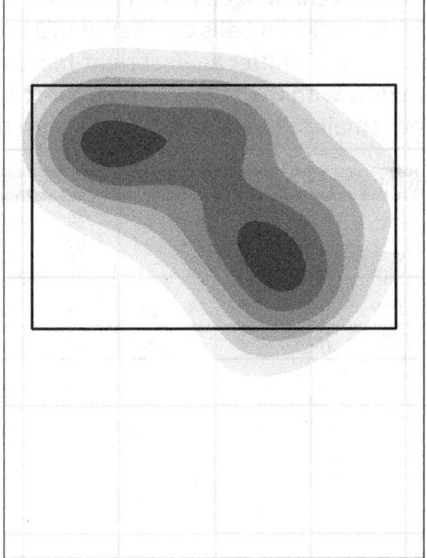

Joey Wendle 2B

Born: 04/26/90   Age: 30   Bats: L   Throws: R
Height: 6'1"   Weight: 200   Origin: Round 6, 2012 Draft (#203 overall)

YEAR	TEAM	LVL	AGE	PA	R	2B	3B	HR	RBI	BB	K	SB	CS	AVG/OBP/SLG
2017	NAS	AAA	27	510	67	29	8	8	54	19	82	13	4	.285/.327/.429
2017	OAK	MLB	27	14	3	1	0	1	5	1	3	0	0	.308/.357/.615
2018	TBA	MLB	28	545	62	33	6	7	61	37	96	16	4	.300/.354/.435
2019	TBA	MLB	29	263	32	13	2	3	19	14	47	8	3	.231/.293/.340
2020	TBA	MLB	30	455	43	22	3	10	47	24	91	8	2	.243/.296/.382

Comparables: Bobby Young, Brandon Phillips, Wil Cordero

What do you get when you cross Ben Zobrist expectations with Sam Fuld's hitting ability? After unexpectedly placing as a finalist for the American League Rookie of the Year award in 2018, Wendle came crashing back to Earth hard. He was hit by a pitch in early April that resulted in a wrist fracture but was not effective even before that injury. Without much threat of power, opposing pitchers challenged him more often in the zone and yet Wendle took 41 percent of his hacks on balls compared to 36 percent the year prior. He remains an average-ish hitter against right-handed pitching and a solid defender up the middle with the ability to play short in a pinch and third base as well. As long as he remains cheap, he has a role with the Rays.

YEAR	TEAM	LVL	AGE	PA	DRC+	VORP	BABIP	BRR	FRAA	WARP
2017	NAS	AAA	27	510	96	26.3	.329	0.6	2B(82): -0.7, 3B(24): 6.3	2.0
2017	OAK	MLB	27	14	93	1.0	.333	-0.2	2B(5): -0.5	0.0
2018	TBA	MLB	28	545	108	33.4	.353	3.7	2B(100): 5.8, 3B(20): 1.4	3.2
2019	TBA	MLB	29	263	81	3.1	.272	-0.2	2B(48): 4.1, 3B(27): -1.1	0.6
2020	TBA	MLB	30	455	82	5.2	.288	1.2	2B 3, 3B 3	1.2

Joey Wendle, continued

Batted Ball Distribution

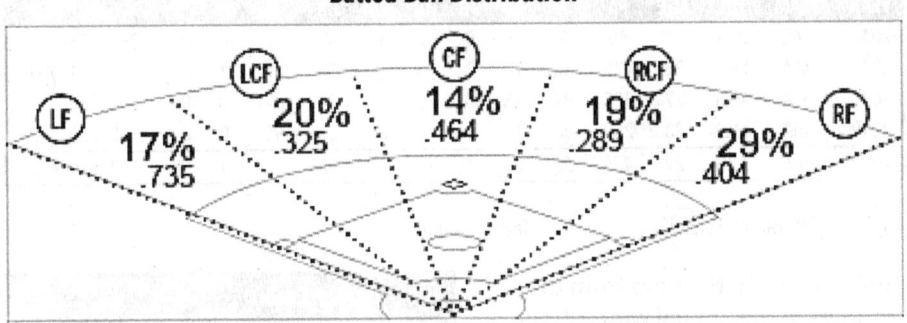

Strike Zone vs LHP **Strike Zone vs RHP**

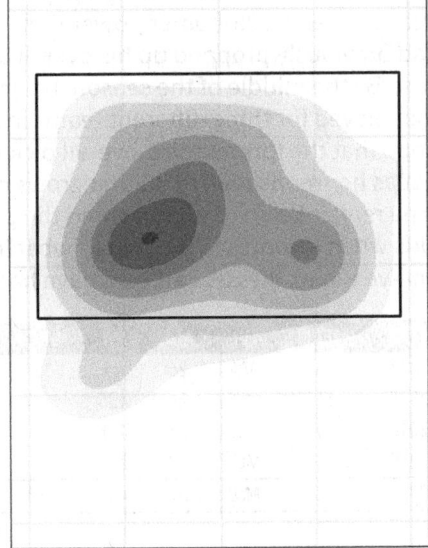

Mike Zunino C

Born: 03/25/91 Age: 29 Bats: R Throws: R
Height: 6'2" Weight: 235 Origin: Round 1, 2012 Draft (#3 overall)

YEAR	TEAM	LVL	AGE	PA	R	2B	3B	HR	RBI	BB	K	SB	CS	AVG/OBP/SLG
2017	TAC	AAA	26	45	7	2	0	5	11	4	5	0	0	.293/.356/.707
2017	SEA	MLB	26	435	52	25	0	25	64	39	160	1	0	.251/.331/.509
2018	SEA	MLB	27	405	37	18	0	20	44	24	150	0	0	.201/.259/.410
2019	TBA	MLB	28	289	30	10	1	9	32	20	98	0	0	.165/.232/.312
2020	TBA	MLB	29	455	52	20	1	23	63	33	163	1	0	.207/.279/.423

Comparables: Bobby Estalella, Mike Napoli, Taylor Teagarden

Zunino came to the Rays from the Mariners in the annual winter trade between the two teams. Home cooking, however, did nothing for the Florida native, as his already abysmal bat sunk to a new low. Making things even worse, the 25-homer power that had previously propped up his overall offense also failed to make the trip back east. By the middle of the season, he had lost his starting gig to an older catcher that played for three different teams in the span of a month. There is always the hope that the former third-overall pick stops flailing at pitches out of the zone, but as he creeps toward 30 that grows more unlikely. The good news for Zunino is he remains a solid hand behind the plate. He is a very good framer and is a plus when it comes to blocking—what led to the Rays bringing him back on a one-year pact. Lesser catchers have had longer careers.

YEAR	TEAM	P. COUNT	FRM RUNS	BLK RUNS	THRW RUNS	TOT RUNS
2017	SEA	16181	10.9	-3.1	-0.6	5.6
2018	SEA	14630	7.5	-1.1	0.4	6.6
2019	TBA	10964	7.0	1.7	1.1	9.8
2020	TBA	19437	12.4	0.0	2.3	14.7

YEAR	TEAM	LVL	AGE	PA	DRC+	VORP	BABIP	BRR	FRAA	WARP
2017	TAC	AAA	26	45	135	9.1	.226	0.6	C(7): 0.8	0.5
2017	SEA	MLB	26	435	109	27.4	.355	-1.4	C(120): 6.3	3.1
2018	SEA	MLB	27	405	83	6.3	.268	-2.2	C(111): 6.4	1.6
2019	TBA	MLB	28	289	57	-1.1	.220	-1.5	C(89): 8.3	0.5
2020	TBA	MLB	29	455	82	9.2	.276	-1.7	C 14	2.4

Mike Zunino, continued

Batted Ball Distribution

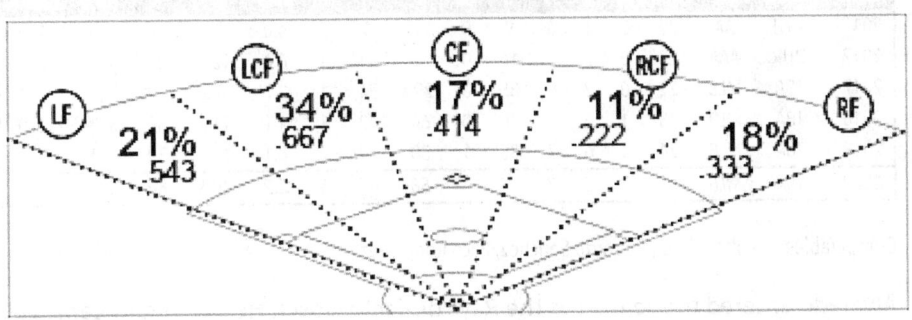

Strike Zone vs LHP **Strike Zone vs RHP**

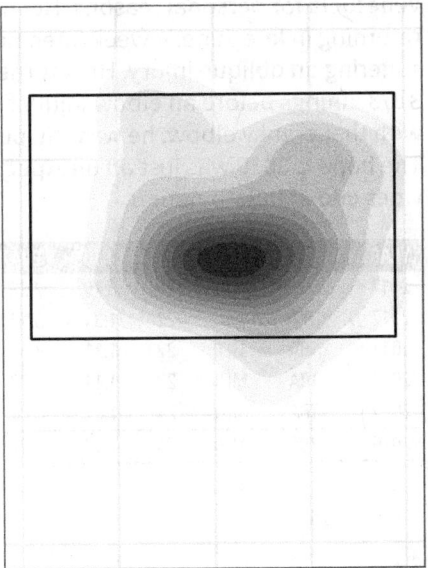

José Alvarado LHP

Born: 05/21/95   Age: 25   Bats: L   Throws: L
Height: 6'2"   Weight: 245   Origin: International Free Agent, 2012

YEAR	TEAM	LVL	AGE	W	L	SV	G	GS	IP	H	HR	BB/9	K/9	K	GB%	BABIP
2017	MNT	AA	22	2	1	0	9	0	11^1	4	1	4.0	11.1	14	78%	.136
2017	DUR	AAA	22	0	2	1	16	0	18^1	11	1	6.4	12.8	26	43%	.244
2017	TBA	MLB	22	0	3	0	35	0	29^2	24	1	2.7	8.8	29	55%	.274
2018	TBA	MLB	23	1	6	8	70	0	64	42	1	4.1	11.2	80	57%	.270
2019	TBA	MLB	24	1	6	7	35	1	30	29	2	8.1	11.7	39	50%	.346
2020	TBA	MLB	25	3	3	7	54	0	58	49	5	5.2	10.7	68	54%	.301

Comparables: Stephen Pryor, Eduardo Sanchez, Paco Rodríguez

Alvarado entered the season as the Rays de-facto closer. He saved four games by April 7 and looked poised for a monster season. The rest of the year sure was scary, but not for the same reasons. The big lefty lost sight of the strike zone and then the team lost sight of him. First, Alvarado left the club to return to Venezuela for personal reasons. He missed nearly a month there before returning in late June. A week later, he gave up eight runs in 3 1/3 innings before suffering an oblique injury. He returned once more only to give up eight walks in 3 1/3 innings before an elbow injury finally ended his season in August. Even with that cranky elbow, he was still pumping a consistent 98 mph until the end. The hope is 2019 was just an unexpected redshirt season presuming his elbow woes end at inflammation.

YEAR	TEAM	LVL	AGE	WHIP	ERA	DRA	WARP	MPH	FB%	WHF	CSP
2017	MNT	AA	22	0.79	2.38	2.70	0.3				
2017	DUR	AAA	22	1.31	3.93	3.32	0.4				
2017	TBA	MLB	22	1.11	3.64	3.44	0.6	100.2	75.8	11.5	48.3
2018	TBA	MLB	23	1.11	2.39	2.65	1.7	100.0	70.5	13.6	49
2019	TBA	MLB	24	1.87	4.80	5.70	-0.1	100.5	79.5	12.6	42.5
2020	TBA	MLB	25	1.43	3.97	4.07	0.7	99.9	76.2	13.2	47.2

José Alvarado, continued

Pitch Shape vs LHH

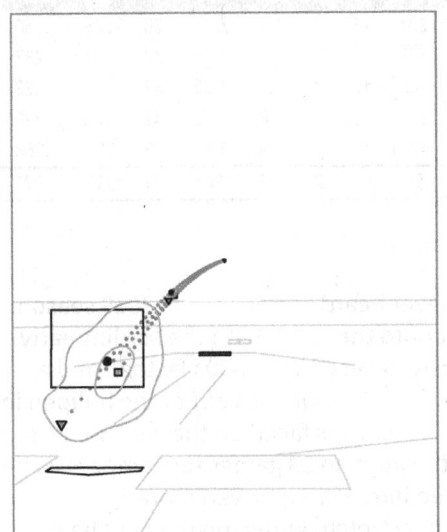

Pitch Shape vs RHH

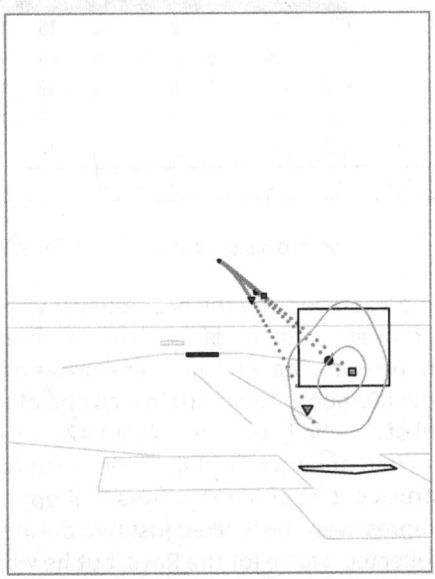

Type	Frequency	Velocity	H Movement	V Movement
● Fastball	25.5%	98.3 [117]	9.4 [89]	-13.1 [107]
☐ Sinker	54.0%	98.9 [133]	11.1 [110]	-13.6 [124]
+ Cutter				
▲ Changeup				
✕ Splitter				
▽ Slider	16.9%	92.8 [136]	-0.9 [83]	-24.7 [124]
◇ Curveball	3.6%	87.3 [129]	-2.2 [79]	-35.5 [125]
⊕ Slow Curveball				
✱ Knuckleball				
▼ Screwball				

Nick Anderson   RHP

Born: 07/05/90   Age: 29   Bats: R   Throws: R
Height: 6'5"   Weight: 195   Origin: Round 32, 2012 Draft (#995 overall)

YEAR	TEAM	LVL	AGE	W	L	SV	G	GS	IP	H	HR	BB/9	K/9	K	GB%	BABIP
2017	FTM	A+	26	2	0	2	15	0	20^1	13	0	1.3	8.9	20	50%	.250
2017	CHT	AA	26	2	1	9	29	0	33^2	19	0	1.9	9.9	37	39%	.237
2018	ROC	AAA	27	8	2	4	39	4	60	49	8	2.8	13.2	88	31%	.323
2019	TBA	MLB	28	3	0	0	23	0	21^1	12	3	0.8	17.3	41	32%	.290
2019	MIA	MLB	28	2	4	1	45	0	43^2	40	5	3.3	14.2	69	28%	.368
2020	TBA	MLB	29	3	2	11	54	0	58	40	7	2.7	14.1	91	31%	.291

Comparables: Chris Smith, Tyler Sturdevant, Aaron Wilkerson

Anderson became the best reliever you never heard of prior to the 2019 season. A former farmhand of the Twins, he burst onto the scene with the Marlins early in the year. The right-hander works exclusively off of a high-90s fastball and a low-80s hook. The tandem was one of the best 1-2 punches out of the bullpen in all of baseball, as he struck out 42 percent of batters faced on the year. He was even better after the July trade north to the Rays. In 23 games for Tampa Bay, he struck out 41 of the 78 hitters that opposed him. Perhaps even more impressively, he walked just two during that stretch. Anderson may not have collected a save for the Rays, but he was the unquestioned relief ace as the team marched toward the playoffs and into the divisional series. Because he was such a late bloomer, he won't even reach arbitration eligibility until the 2022 season.

YEAR	TEAM	LVL	AGE	WHIP	ERA	DRA	WARP	MPH	FB%	WHF	CSP
2017	FTM	A+	26	0.79	0.89	2.39	0.6				
2017	CHT	AA	26	0.77	1.07	2.17	1.1				
2018	ROC	AAA	27	1.13	3.30	3.62	1.1				
2019	TBA	MLB	28	0.66	2.11	0.75	1.1	98.0	69	26	53.8
2019	MIA	MLB	28	1.28	3.92	3.41	0.9	97.5	55.9	18.2	48
2020	TBA	MLB	29	0.99	2.28	2.70	1.6	97.0	59.9	20.5	49.7

Nick Anderson, continued

Pitch Shape vs LHH

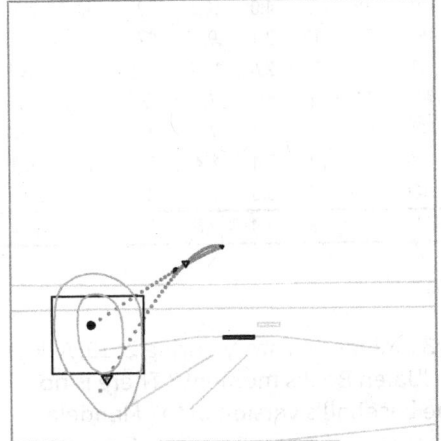

Pitch Shape vs RHH

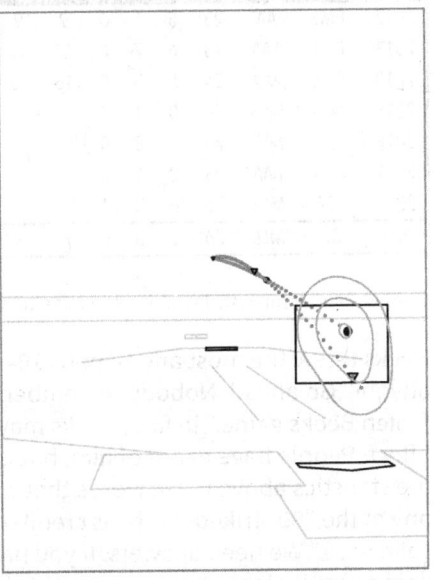

Type	Frequency	Velocity	H Movement	V Movement
● Fastball	59.9%	96.4 [111]	-4.8 [109]	-9.2 [118]
☐ Sinker				
+ Cutter				
▲ Changeup				
✕ Splitter				
▽ Slider	40.1%	83.4 [96]	1.6 [86]	-37.4 [87]
◇ Curveball				
⊕ Slow Curveball				
✱ Knuckleball				
▼ Screwball				

Jalen Beeks LHP

Born: 07/10/93   Age: 26   Bats: L   Throws: L
Height: 5'11"   Weight: 200   Origin: Round 12, 2014 Draft (#374 overall)

YEAR	TEAM	LVL	AGE	W	L	SV	G	GS	IP	H	HR	BB/9	K/9	K	GB%	BABIP
2017	PME	AA	23	5	1	0	9	9	49^1	35	3	4.0	10.6	58	51%	.276
2017	PAW	AAA	23	6	7	0	17	17	95^2	86	10	3.1	9.1	97	45%	.291
2018	PAW	AAA	24	5	5	0	16	16	87^1	70	10	2.6	12.1	117	41%	.299
2018	BOS	MLB	24	0	1	0	2	1	6^1	11	1	5.7	7.1	5	33%	.435
2018	TBA	MLB	24	5	0	0	12	0	44^1	41	5	4.1	7.5	37	51%	.288
2019	DUR	AAA	25	0	1	0	3	3	10^2	8	2	3.4	8.4	10	39%	.231
2019	TBA	MLB	25	6	3	1	33	3	104^1	115	12	3.5	7.7	89	48%	.328
2020	TBA	MLB	26	3	3	0	52	3	61	61	9	3.4	7.8	53	46%	.294

Comparables: John Gast, José Álvarez, Adalberto Mejía

Beeks threw the most anonymous 104 1/3 innings in history during 2019. Ask anyone. Go ahead. Nobody remembers a "Jalen Beeks moment." There is no "Jalen Beeks game." In fact, Beeks may be baseball's version of the Mandela Effect. People have heard of him, but is there proof he really exists? Sure, there are statistics above these words that say he does, but did you actually witness any of the "89 strikeouts" he is credited with? Who hit the 12 home runs he "allowed?" We need answers. If you have any vivid memories of Beeks actually being a major league player—or even better—visual evidence, please direct them to the estate of Robert Stack.

YEAR	TEAM	LVL	AGE	WHIP	ERA	DRA	WARP	MPH	FB%	WHF	CSP
2017	PME	AA	23	1.16	2.19	2.94	1.3				
2017	PAW	AAA	23	1.24	3.86	4.17	1.6				
2018	PAW	AAA	24	1.09	2.89	3.33	2.2				
2018	BOS	MLB	24	2.37	12.79	7.48	-0.2	93.9	42.5	9.5	42.7
2018	TBA	MLB	24	1.38	4.47	5.18	-0.1	93.9	42.5	13.1	45
2019	DUR	AAA	25	1.12	4.22	3.94	0.3				
2019	TBA	MLB	25	1.49	4.31	6.89	-1.7	94.6	43.6	11	46.3
2020	TBA	MLB	26	1.38	4.55	4.69	0.4	94.0	44.1	11.7	46.4

Jalen Beeks, continued

Pitch Shape vs LHH

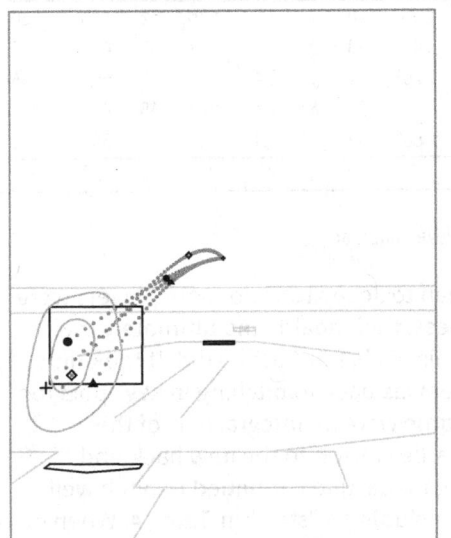

Pitch Shape vs RHH

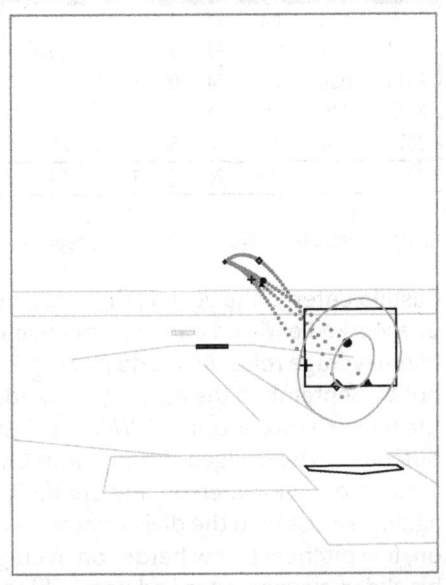

Type	Frequency	Velocity	H Movement	V Movement
● Fastball	43.5%	92.6 [101]	4.9 [109]	-13.9 [105]
☐ Sinker				
+ Cutter	5.9%	86.6 [87]	-0.5 [92]	-26.2 [92]
▲ Changeup	31.7%	87.7 [109]	14 [87]	-25.4 [106]
✕ Splitter				
▽ Slider				
◇ Curveball	18.8%	75.5 [90]	-9.1 [107]	-55.9 [82]
✦ Slow Curveball				
✱ Knuckleball				
▼ Screwball				

Diego Castillo   RHP

Born: 01/18/94   Age: 26   Bats: R   Throws: R
Height: 6'3"   Weight: 250   Origin: International Free Agent, 2014

YEAR	TEAM	LVL	AGE	W	L	SV	G	GS	IP	H	HR	BB/9	K/9	K	GB%	BABIP
2017	MNT	AA	23	1	3	8	21	0	29	20	1	2.2	9.9	32	61%	.250
2017	DUR	AAA	23	3	2	7	30	1	42^2	38	2	2.7	12.2	58	40%	.353
2018	DUR	AAA	24	0	1	4	19	0	26^1	15	1	2.4	10.9	32	59%	.246
2018	TBA	MLB	24	4	2	0	43	11	56^2	36	6	2.9	10.3	65	46%	.229
2019	TBA	MLB	25	5	8	8	65	6	68^2	59	8	3.4	10.6	81	56%	.300
2020	TBA	MLB	26	3	3	4	54	0	58	48	6	3.3	10.9	70	52%	.294

Comparables: Michael Tonkin, Chandler Shepherd, Jaye Chapman

Castillo entered the year as the setup man to José Alvarado. Both players were overworked early on and lost effectiveness, their health and ultimately their high-leverage roles. Alvarado never got his back, but Castillo did. It took time, but by September, the burly right-hander was back to pitching in key spots for the Rays. His six outs in the Wild Card Game were an integral part of the outcome as he bridged the gap from Charlie Morton to the new back-end tandem of Nick Anderson and Emilio Pagán. Castillo continued to pitch well against Houston in the divisional series including a "start" in Game 4. When he is on, few pitchers throw harder on average. The high-octane fastball is great, but his slider is even better and part of his resurgence was due to a month-over-month increase in breaking balls—peaking with a nice 69-percent usage rate in September. The big man will be counted on to get big outs once again this year.

YEAR	TEAM	LVL	AGE	WHIP	ERA	DRA	WARP	MPH	FB%	WHF	CSP
2017	MNT	AA	23	0.93	1.86	2.44	0.8				
2017	DUR	AAA	23	1.20	3.38	4.23	0.5				
2018	DUR	AAA	24	0.84	1.03	2.21	0.9				
2018	TBA	MLB	24	0.95	3.18	3.70	0.9	101.0	54.1	14	48.9
2019	TBA	MLB	25	1.24	3.41	3.41	1.5	100.2	48.5	14.8	48.2
2020	TBA	MLB	26	1.20	3.24	3.54	1.0	100.1	51.6	14.7	49.4

Diego Castillo, continued

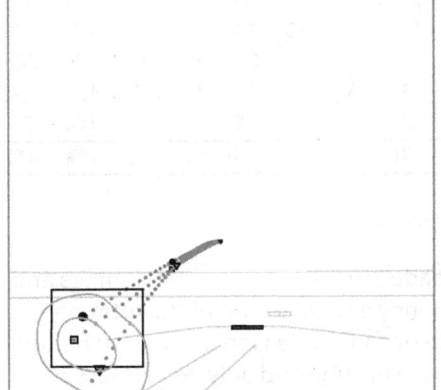
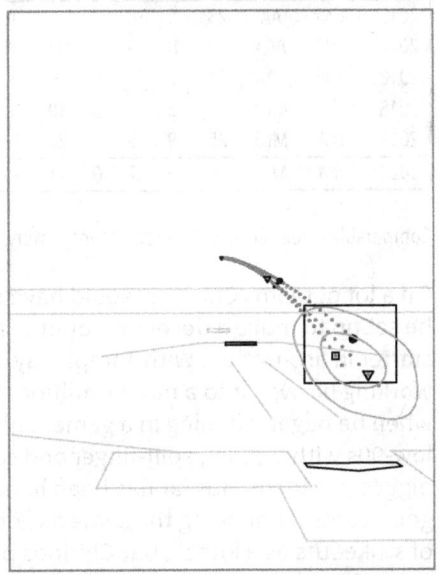

Type	Frequency	Velocity	H Movement	V Movement
● Fastball	12.2%	98.7 [118]	-9.8 [87]	-14 [105]
☐ Sinker	36.3%	98.5 [130]	-14.4 [89]	-17.5 [110]
+ Cutter				
▲ Changeup				
✕ Splitter				
▽ Slider	51.5%	89 [120]	4.9 [99]	-29.3 [111]
◇ Curveball				
⊕ Slow Curveball				
✱ Knuckleball				
▼ Screwball				

Yonny Chirinos   RHP

Born: 12/26/93   Age: 26   Bats: R   Throws: R
Height: 6'2"   Weight: 240   Origin: International Free Agent, 2012

YEAR	TEAM	LVL	AGE	W	L	SV	G	GS	IP	H	HR	BB/9	K/9	K	GB%	BABIP
2017	MNT	AA	23	1	0	0	4	4	27^1	22	5	1.3	6.9	21	58%	.233
2017	DUR	AAA	23	12	5	0	23	22	141	116	10	1.4	7.7	120	52%	.270
2018	DUR	AAA	24	0	2	0	8	8	30^2	35	7	2.1	9.1	31	50%	.326
2018	TBA	MLB	24	5	5	0	18	7	89^2	84	7	2.5	7.5	75	45%	.298
2019	TBA	MLB	25	9	5	0	26	18	133^1	112	23	1.9	7.7	114	44%	.246
2020	TBA	MLB	26	8	7	0	44	19	131	122	18	2.5	8.0	116	45%	.282

Comparables: Joe Musgrove, Jordan Montgomery, Trevor Oaks

On a lot of teams Chirinos would have made 30 starts, pitched 175 innings and be set up to make a decent amount of money as a back-end of the rotation starter in arbitration. With Tampa Bay, he began the season as a hybrid before working his way into a more traditional role in June and July. Regardless of when he began pitching in a game, Chirinos was effective. He works in the low-90s with a slider, split-finger and solid control of the three-pitch mix. His biggest problem thus far has been home runs. This gets into the discussion of good control not being the same as good command. Some may look at the lack of strikeouts as a knock, but Chirinos pitches to contact and lives in the zone more than the average pitcher. This allowed him to average just under 15 pitches per inning. Effective and efficient aren't sexy, but it gets the job done most of the time. That's Chirinos in a honey nut shell.

YEAR	TEAM	LVL	AGE	WHIP	ERA	DRA	WARP	MPH	FB%	WHF	CSP
2017	MNT	AA	23	0.95	2.63	3.78	0.5				
2017	DUR	AAA	23	0.98	2.74	3.00	4.2				
2018	DUR	AAA	24	1.37	5.28	5.92	-0.1				
2018	TBA	MLB	24	1.22	3.51	4.23	0.9	96.4	63.1	12.2	49.8
2019	TBA	MLB	25	1.05	3.85	4.29	2.0	96.4	56.8	11.1	48.1
2020	TBA	MLB	26	1.21	3.66	4.00	2.2	96.0	60.1	11.7	49.7

Yonny Chirinos, continued

Pitch Shape vs LHH

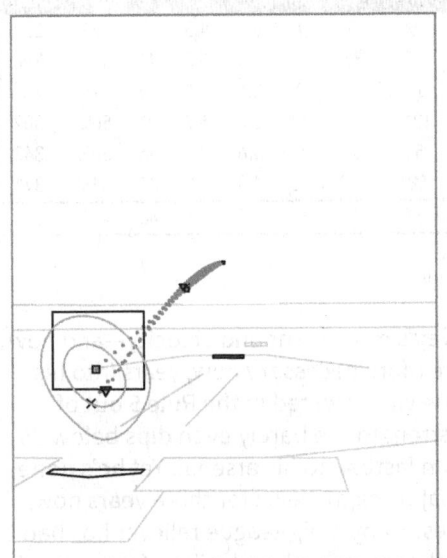

Pitch Shape vs RHH

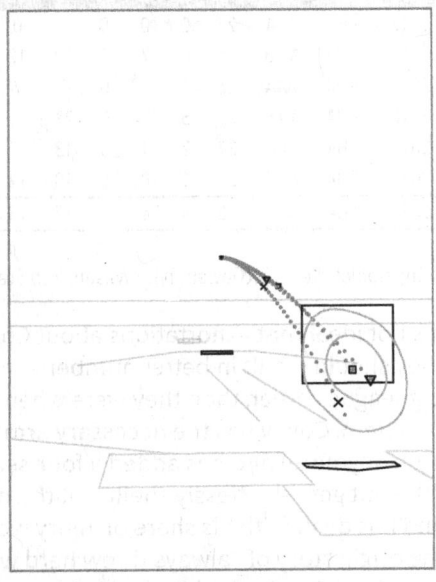

Type	Frequency	Velocity	H Movement	V Movement
● Fastball				
□ Sinker	55.9%	94.2 [108]	-14.9 [85]	-18 [108]
+ Cutter				
▲ Changeup				
✕ Splitter	21.7%	86.1 [104]	-7.8 [101]	-29.8 [98]
▽ Slider	21.5%	88 [115]	3.5 [94]	-26.3 [120]
◇ Curveball				
✦ Slow Curveball				
✱ Knuckleball				
▼ Screwball				

Dylan Covey   RHP

Born: 08/14/91   Age: 28   Bats: R   Throws: R
Height: 6'1"   Weight: 220   Origin: Round 4, 2013 Draft (#131 overall)

YEAR	TEAM	LVL	AGE	W	L	SV	G	GS	IP	H	HR	BB/9	K/9	K	GB%	BABIP
2017	CHR	AAA	25	0	0	0	2	0	6	5	1	1.5	4.5	3	58%	.222
2017	CHA	MLB	25	0	7	0	18	12	70	83	20	4.4	5.3	41	49%	.296
2018	CHR	AAA	26	3	1	0	7	7	38²	32	3	3.5	8.1	35	57%	.282
2018	CHA	MLB	26	5	14	0	27	21	121²	129	13	3.8	6.7	91	56%	.302
2019	CHR	AAA	27	2	1	0	13	11	51	59	6	1.6	8.1	46	56%	.342
2019	CHA	MLB	27	1	8	0	18	12	58²	75	12	4.3	6.3	41	44%	.321
2020	CHA	MLB	28	4	4	0	13	13	65	77	13	3.5	6.4	46	49%	.312

Comparables: Kevin McGowan, Tyler Wilson, Rob Scahill

It's not ideal that exhortations about Covey's movement and velocity—and how they should result in better numbers—are more necessary now, years into his big-league career, than they were when he was selected in the Rule 5 out of Double-A. Covey has the necessary arm strength (he barely even dips below 95 mph anymore) and has added a four-seam fastball to his arsenal. Yet he's done little but get relentlessly shelled at the major-league level for three years now, and has dealt with his share of injury woes. Many a big-league reliever has had the origin story of "always threw hard with movement" and still self-actualized somehow. For Covey, his awakening may require that the White Sox stop having him start.

YEAR	TEAM	LVL	AGE	WHIP	ERA	DRA	WARP	MPH	FB%	WHF	CSP
2017	CHR	AAA	25	1.00	3.00	4.55	0.0				
2017	CHA	MLB	25	1.67	7.71	7.88	-1.9	95.0	60.5	6.8	45.5
2018	CHR	AAA	26	1.22	2.33	3.98	0.7				
2018	CHA	MLB	26	1.49	5.18	5.15	0.2	96.3	61.4	7.8	49.6
2019	CHR	AAA	27	1.33	2.82	3.83	1.4				
2019	CHA	MLB	27	1.76	7.98	7.92	-1.4	96.5	49.8	8.3	49.3
2020	CHA	MLB	28	1.58	5.98	5.76	-0.1	95.5	58.1	7.8	48.8

Dylan Covey, continued

Pitch Shape vs LHH	Pitch Shape vs RHH
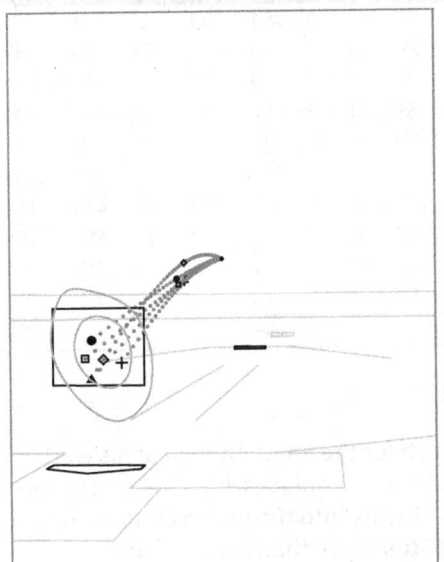	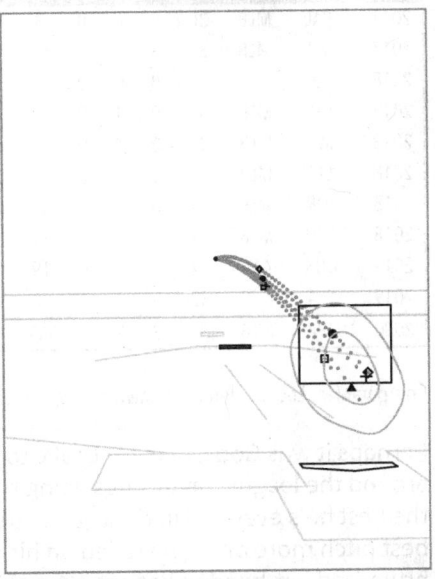

Type	Frequency	Velocity	H Movement	V Movement
● Fastball	18.3%	94.8 [107]	-3.7 [114]	-13.8 [106]
□ Sinker	31.5%	94.7 [111]	-10.3 [115]	-15.5 [117]
+ Cutter	22.0%	91.3 [116]	2.8 [106]	-20.6 [113]
▲ Changeup	18.2%	86.1 [103]	-7.5 [117]	-28.4 [97]
✕ Splitter				
▽ Slider				
◇ Curveball	7.7%	81.9 [111]	3.4 [83]	-40.5 [115]
⊕ Slow Curveball				
✱ Knuckleball				
▼ Screwball				

Rays Player Analysis - 67

Oliver Drake RHP

Born: 01/13/87 Age: 33 Bats: R Throws: R
Height: 6'4" Weight: 215 Origin: Round 43, 2008 Draft (#1286 overall)

YEAR	TEAM	LVL	AGE	W	L	SV	G	GS	IP	H	HR	BB/9	K/9	K	GB%	BABIP
2017	BAL	MLB	30	0	0	0	3	0	3^1	6	0	8.1	8.1	3	67%	.500
2017	MIL	MLB	30	3	5	1	61	0	52^2	57	6	3.8	10.1	59	49%	.349
2018	SLC	AAA	31	0	0	0	6	0	7^2	3	0	1.2	9.4	8	71%	.176
2018	LAA	MLB	31	0	1	0	8	0	8^2	15	2	1.0	8.3	8	39%	.448
2018	MIL	MLB	31	1	0	0	11	0	12^2	14	0	5.7	10.7	15	57%	.400
2018	CLE	MLB	31	0	0	0	4	0	4^1	7	0	2.1	8.3	4	31%	.438
2018	TOR	MLB	31	0	0	0	2	0	1^2	4	0	0.0	10.8	2	43%	.571
2018	MIN	MLB	31	0	0	0	19	0	20^1	12	2	3.1	9.7	22	55%	.204
2019	DUR	AAA	32	1	2	6	19	2	23^2	20	2	2.7	15.2	40	51%	.400
2019	TBA	MLB	32	5	2	2	50	0	56	36	9	3.1	11.2	70	52%	.225
2020	TBA	MLB	33	3	2	0	48	0	51	40	6	3.4	10.8	61	51%	.283

Comparables: Louis Coleman, Shawn Kelley, James Hoyt

Perhaps it was God's plan for Drake to pitch for the Rays. After all of his work around the league, and things going badly in other places, his 2019 season was the best he's ever had in the big leagues. Buying into the motto of throwing your best pitch more often, he relied on his splitter more than ever and just brutalized left-handed batters, who collectively hit .147/.163/.196 against him. Considering Tampa Bay's pitching philosophy requires the bullpen hotline to bling more than most teams, Drake was seemingly throwing nonstop and tied a career-high with 56 innings pitched despite making his first major-league appearance after Memorial Day. After passing through five other organizations in 2018, it looks like he's finally found a home and a role that suits him best in Tampa.

YEAR	TEAM	LVL	AGE	WHIP	ERA	DRA	WARP	MPH	FB%	WHF	CSP
2017	BAL	MLB	30	2.70	8.10	6.84	-0.1	93.5	47.6	11	43.7
2017	MIL	MLB	30	1.50	4.44	4.35	0.5	93.8	51.6	13	45.1
2018	SLC	AAA	31	0.52	1.17	2.17	0.3				
2018	LAA	MLB	31	1.85	5.19	3.11	0.2	94.4	47.1	15	49.1
2018	MIL	MLB	31	1.74	6.39	2.52	0.4	94.6	49.3	13.5	50.5
2018	CLE	MLB	31	1.85	12.46	2.59	0.1	94.2	48.1	14.3	45.6
2018	TOR	MLB	31	2.40	16.20	1.95	0.1	94.1	58.3	8.3	52.2
2018	MIN	MLB	31	0.93	2.21	3.40	0.4	93.9	40.6	13.6	45.5
2019	DUR	AAA	32	1.14	4.94	2.46	0.9				
2019	TBA	MLB	32	0.98	3.21	3.12	1.4	95.1	40.7	17.7	48.3
2020	TBA	MLB	33	1.17	2.96	3.29	1.1	93.4	44.6	15	46.7

Oliver Drake, continued

Pitch Shape vs LHH	Pitch Shape vs RHH
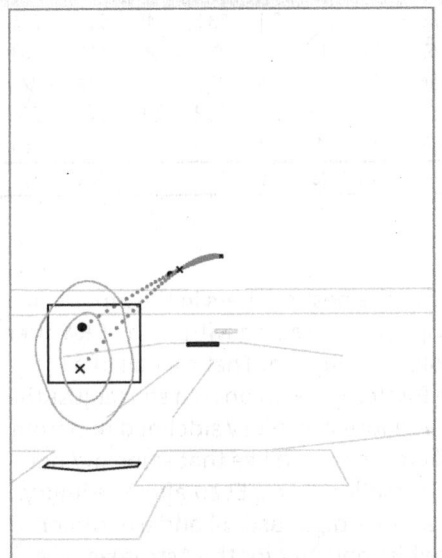	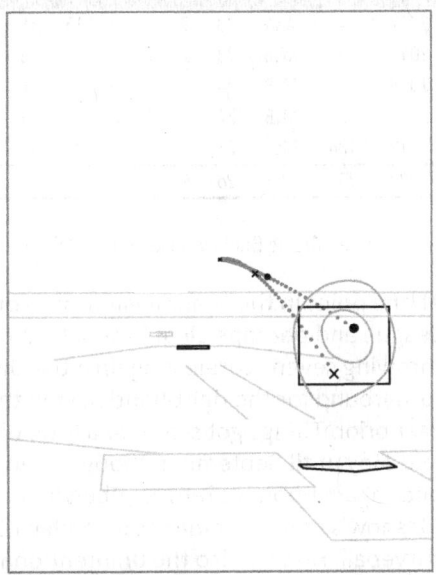

Type	Frequency	Velocity	H Movement	V Movement
● Fastball	40.7%	93.9 [104]	1.4 [137]	-11.8 [111]
□ Sinker				
+ Cutter				
▲ Changeup				
✕ Splitter	58.0%	84.3 [96]	-1.8 [123]	-31.6 [92]
▽ Slider				
◇ Curveball				
⊕ Slow Curveball				
✱ Knuckleball				
▼ Screwball				

Tyler Glasnow   RHP

Born: 08/23/93   Age: 26   Bats: L   Throws: R
Height: 6'8"   Weight: 230   Origin: Round 5, 2011 Draft (#152 overall)

YEAR	TEAM	LVL	AGE	W	L	SV	G	GS	IP	H	HR	BB/9	K/9	K	GB%	BABIP
2017	IND	AAA	23	9	2	0	15	15	93^1	57	6	3.1	13.5	140	50%	.276
2017	PIT	MLB	23	2	7	0	15	13	62	81	13	6.4	8.1	56	44%	.358
2018	PIT	MLB	24	1	2	0	34	0	56	47	5	5.5	11.6	72	57%	.321
2018	TBA	MLB	24	1	5	0	11	11	55^2	42	10	3.1	10.3	64	44%	.248
2019	TBA	MLB	25	6	1	0	12	12	60^2	40	4	2.1	11.3	76	50%	.265
2020	TBA	MLB	26	9	9	0	28	28	140	124	18	3.9	11.4	178	46%	.312

Comparables: Archie Bradley, José Berríos, Jake Faria

At one point in the year, Glasnow was one of the best pitchers in the American League and perhaps all of baseball—sitting on a 6-0 record with a 1.47 ERA after throwing seven scoreless against the Orioles on May 3rd. That's a hell of a turnaround for the right-hander, who the Pirates gave up on as a starter just the year prior. Things got scary for a little bit as a forearm injury sidelined him from mid-May until September, though he looked very much like that same pitcher once again upon his return, albeit in much smaller doses. Even after the injury, Glasnow's stuff remained top notch with a triple-digit fastball and a hammer curveball. He was also the unintentional whistleblower for the Astros sign-stealing endeavor when it appeared as if the Astros knew was he was going to throw even before he did in the ALDS. He enters 2020 as one of three potential aces for a club looking to advance to the LCS for the first time in a dozen years.

YEAR	TEAM	LVL	AGE	WHIP	ERA	DRA	WARP	MPH	FB%	WHF	CSP
2017	IND	AAA	23	0.95	1.93	2.20	3.6				
2017	PIT	MLB	23	2.02	7.69	8.17	-1.8	97.6	64.7	8.6	46.9
2018	PIT	MLB	24	1.45	4.34	2.88	1.4	99.7	72.5	12.4	46.3
2018	TBA	MLB	24	1.10	4.20	3.64	0.9	99.3	68.2	13.2	48.5
2019	TBA	MLB	25	0.89	1.78	2.77	2.0	99.8	67.3	12.4	50.2
2020	TBA	MLB	26	1.32	3.91	4.09	2.3	98.8	69.5	11.9	49.3

Tyler Glasnow, continued

Pitch Shape vs LHH
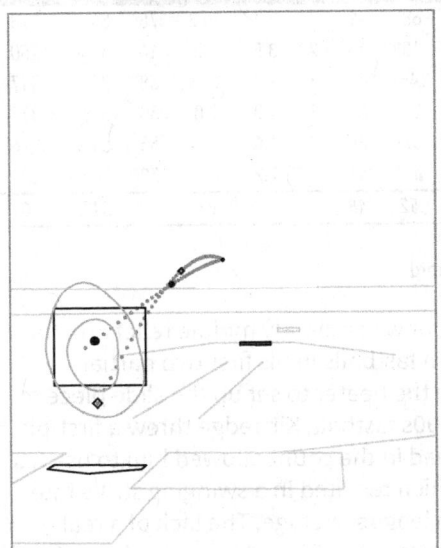

Pitch Shape vs RHH
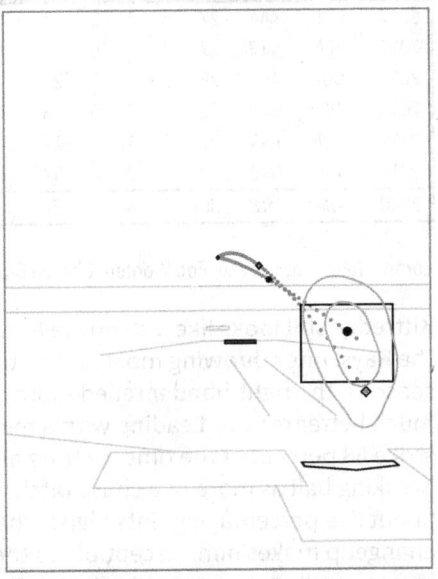

Type	Frequency	Velocity	H Movement	V Movement
● Fastball	67.3%	97.7 [115]	0.2 [131]	-11.9 [111]
☐ Sinker				
+ Cutter				
▲ Changeup	3.5%	93.5 [130]	-9.4 [108]	-20.7 [120]
✕ Splitter				
▽ Slider				
◇ Curveball	29.2%	84.2 [119]	5.2 [91]	-50.6 [94]
✦ Slow Curveball				
✱ Knuckleball				
▼ Screwball				

Andrew Kittredge RHP

Born: 03/17/90 Age: 30 Bats: R Throws: R
Height: 6'1" Weight: 235 Origin: Round 45, 2008 Draft (#1360 overall)

YEAR	TEAM	LVL	AGE	W	L	SV	G	GS	IP	H	HR	BB/9	K/9	K	GB%	BABIP
2017	DUR	AAA	27	6	1	2	41	2	68^1	49	2	2.1	10.3	78	54%	.278
2017	TBA	MLB	27	0	1	0	15	0	15^1	13	2	3.5	8.2	14	50%	.250
2018	DUR	AAA	28	6	0	2	21	1	46	41	3	2.3	11.3	58	39%	.317
2018	TBA	MLB	28	3	2	0	33	3	38^1	54	7	4.0	7.0	30	51%	.373
2019	DUR	AAA	29	2	1	6	27	1	37^1	24	3	1.4	13.3	55	51%	.276
2019	TBA	MLB	29	1	0	0	37	7	49^2	51	7	2.2	10.5	58	50%	.336
2020	TBA	MLB	30	3	4	0	37	13	52	48	6	2.8	9.9	57	51%	.307

Comparables: Josh Lueke, Rob Wooten, Chasen Bradford

Kittredge still looks like a sleepy fellow, but was a steady middle relief arm for the Rays. After throwing more sliders than fastballs in his first two partial seasons, the right-hander relied more on the heater to set up the slide piece to much better results. Leading with a mid-90s fastball, Kittredge threw a first-pitch strike 68 percent of the time. Getting ahead in the count allowed him to use his breaking ball as more of a chase pitch which resulted in a swinging strike rate about five percentage points higher than league average. The lack of a real changeup makes him susceptible to the platoon split, and he typically worked in low-to-medium leverage situations. That said, when you rely on the bullpen as much as Tampa Bay does, the 2019 version of Kittredge is a nice piece of an expanding puzzle.

YEAR	TEAM	LVL	AGE	WHIP	ERA	DRA	WARP	MPH	FB%	WHF	CSP
2017	DUR	AAA	27	0.95	1.45	2.67	2.0				
2017	TBA	MLB	27	1.24	1.76	3.25	0.3	96.4	29	13.1	48.4
2018	DUR	AAA	28	1.15	2.74	3.39	0.9				
2018	TBA	MLB	28	1.85	7.75	6.06	-0.5	95.6	39.8	10.5	47.1
2019	DUR	AAA	29	0.80	1.93	1.32	1.8				
2019	TBA	MLB	29	1.27	4.17	3.73	0.9	96.5	58.1	16.4	43.6
2020	TBA	MLB	30	1.25	3.60	3.88	0.9	95.4	48.7	14	45.8

Andrew Kittredge, continued

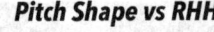
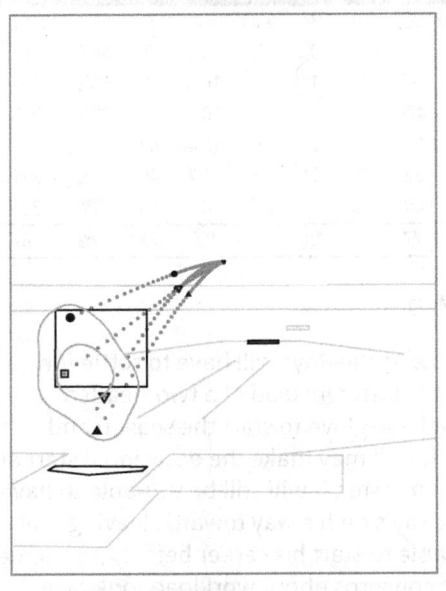
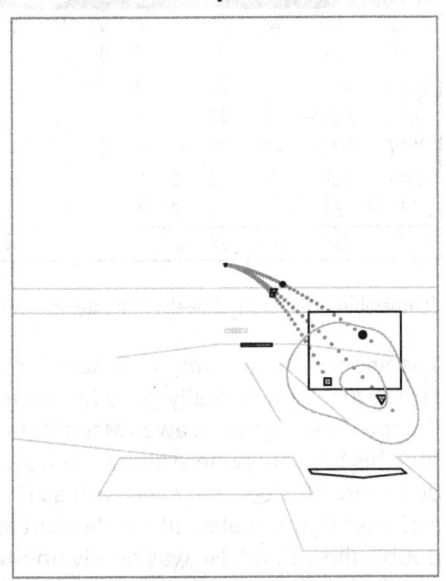

Type	Frequency	Velocity	H Movement	V Movement
● Fastball	17.9%	95.5 [109]	-7.9 [96]	-11.5 [112]
☐ Sinker	40.2%	95.1 [113]	-15.5 [82]	-18.1 [108]
+ Cutter				
▲ Changeup	4.5%	86.1 [103]	-6.4 [122]	-30.7 [90]
✕ Splitter				
▽ Slider	37.4%	88.5 [117]	6.6 [107]	-29.9 [109]
◇ Curveball				
⊕ Slow Curveball				
✱ Knuckleball				
▼ Screwball				

Rays Player Analysis - 73

Brendan McKay LHP

Born: 12/18/95   Age: 24   Bats: L   Throws: L
Height: 6'2"   Weight: 212   Origin: Round 1, 2017 Draft (#4 overall)

YEAR	TEAM	LVL	AGE	W	L	SV	G	GS	IP	H	HR	BB/9	K/9	K	GB%	BABIP
2017	HUD	A-	21	1	0	0	6	6	20	10	3	2.2	9.4	21	53%	.159
2018	RAY	RK	22	0	0	0	2	2	6	2	0	1.5	13.5	9	58%	.167
2018	BGR	A	22	2	0	0	6	6	24^2	8	1	0.7	14.6	40	63%	.167
2018	PCH	A+	22	3	2	0	11	9	47^2	45	2	2.1	10.2	54	39%	.350
2019	MNT	AA	23	3	0	0	8	7	41^2	25	2	1.9	13.4	62	44%	.280
2019	DUR	AAA	23	3	0	0	7	6	32	17	1	2.5	11.2	40	49%	.229
2019	TBA	MLB	23	2	4	0	13	11	49	53	8	2.9	10.3	56	37%	.331
2020	TBA	MLB	24	5	5	0	18	18	77	73	12	2.9	8.6	73	39%	.287

Comparables: Dan Straily, Rogelio Armenteros, Joe Musgrove

The Shohei Ohtani comps can stop for now as the Rays will have to settle for McKay just being a really good left-handed starter instead of a two-headed dragon. The Rays took away McKay's first base glove to start the season and then his bat somewhere along the way. He still may make the occasional start at designated hitter—and even with a 26-man roster, it will still be valuable to have a pitcher that can also hit a little—but McKay's on his way towards leaving that double life behind. He was nearly unhittable to start his career before the league caught up to him. By the end of the year, concerns about workload took over and he didn't throw over 65 pitches in an appearance after mid-August. Despite the ups and downs, McKay showed stuff and poise that makes him a potential number two or three starter. He has a four-pitch mix led by a low-to-mid 90s fastball and a true, plus curveball. Developing command led to some home run issues at the highest level, but he has the ability to repeat and turn that into a strength. The Rays may play some games early in the year with regards to service time and innings totals, but McKay should toss his most important pitches for Tampa Bay in 2020.

YEAR	TEAM	LVL	AGE	WHIP	ERA	DRA	WARP	MPH	FB%	WHF	CSP
2017	HUD	A-	21	0.75	1.80	2.68	0.6				
2018	RAY	RK	22	0.50	1.50	0.71	0.3				
2018	BGR	A	22	0.41	1.09	1.44	1.1				
2018	PCH	A+	22	1.17	3.21	3.90	0.7				
2019	MNT	AA	23	0.82	1.30	2.51	1.2				
2019	DUR	AAA	23	0.81	0.84	1.54	1.6				
2019	TBA	MLB	23	1.41	5.14	5.79	0.0	95.6	57.1	11.6	50.4
2020	TBA	MLB	24	1.27	4.12	4.41	1.0	95.4	58.8	12	51.9

Brendan McKay, continued

Pitch Shape vs LHH

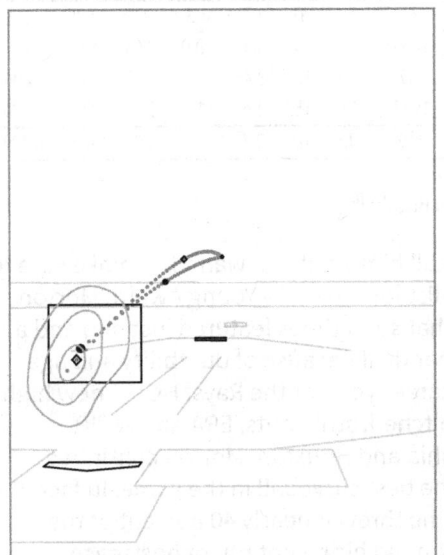

Pitch Shape vs RHH

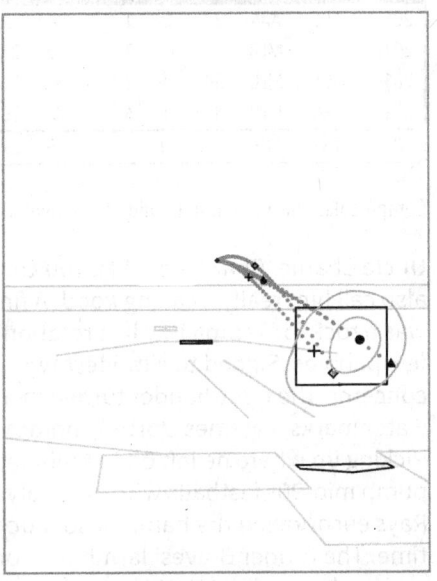

Type	Frequency	Velocity	H Movement	V Movement
● Fastball	57.1%	93.9 [104]	8.3 [94]	-12.8 [108]
☐ Sinker				
+ Cutter	13.0%	89.3 [104]	0.6 [86]	-21.3 [110]
▲ Changeup	3.8%	86.8 [106]	11.1 [100]	-20.8 [119]
✗ Splitter				
▽ Slider				
◇ Curveball	26.2%	81.9 [111]	-7 [98]	-44.4 [107]
⊕ Slow Curveball				
✶ Knuckleball				
▼ Screwball				

Charlie Morton   RHP

Born: 11/12/83   Age: 36   Bats: R   Throws: R
Height: 6'5"   Weight: 215   Origin: Round 3, 2002 Draft (#95 overall)

YEAR	TEAM	LVL	AGE	W	L	SV	G	GS	IP	H	HR	BB/9	K/9	K	GB%	BABIP
2017	FRE	AAA	33	0	1	0	2	2	6	4	1	3.0	4.5	3	71%	.188
2017	HOU	MLB	33	14	7	0	25	25	146²	125	14	3.1	10.0	163	53%	.295
2018	HOU	MLB	34	15	3	0	30	30	167	130	18	3.4	10.8	201	49%	.284
2019	TBA	MLB	35	16	6	0	33	33	194²	154	15	2.6	11.1	240	48%	.298
2020	TBA	MLB	36	11	9	0	29	29	169	142	18	3.1	11.0	206	48%	.299

Comparables: Jason Hammel, Todd Stottlemyre, Clay Buchholz

Uncle Charlie. Chaz Moe. CFM. You can call him what you want, but make sure to also call him really freaking good. A finalist for the AL Cy Young Award, Morton was a rock for Tampa Bay in a rotation that sometimes featured just him and a few pebbles. Signed to a modest two-year deal because of durability and age concerns, the right-hander turned in a career year for the Rays. He set new high-water marks in games started, innings pitched, strikeouts, ERA and WHIP. Picking up where he left off in Philadelphia and Houston, Morton continued to pump mid-90s fastballs with arguably the best curveball in the game. In fact, the Rays encouraged the hammer so much, he threw it nearly 40 percent of the time. The former Braves' farmhand continued his recent run of postseason success by tossing 10 additional frames and allowing just one earned run in the process. Obviously, the Rays would prefer their younger arms to shoulder more of the load in 2020 with Cholly, Chip, Ground Chuck Morton being a solid pillar of support.

YEAR	TEAM	LVL	AGE	WHIP	ERA	DRA	WARP	MPH	FB%	WHF	CSP
2017	FRE	AAA	33	1.00	1.50	4.31	0.1				
2017	HOU	MLB	33	1.19	3.62	3.92	2.7	97.1	65.6	11.5	48.6
2018	HOU	MLB	34	1.16	3.13	3.68	3.1	97.9	63.4	12.8	48.3
2019	TBA	MLB	35	1.08	3.05	2.96	5.9	96.4	50.2	14	50
2020	TBA	MLB	36	1.18	3.33	3.58	3.7	95.7	56.5	12.8	48

Charlie Morton, continued

Pitch Shape vs LHH

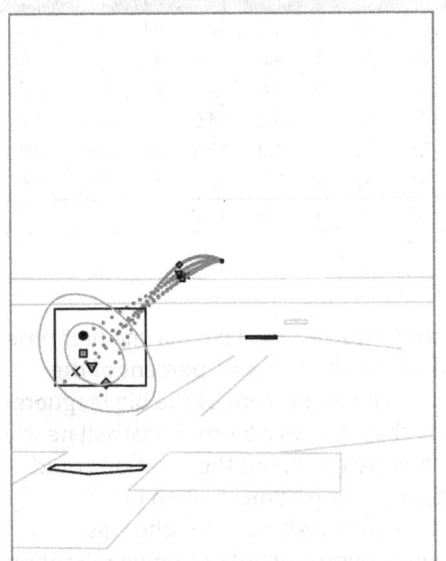

Pitch Shape vs RHH

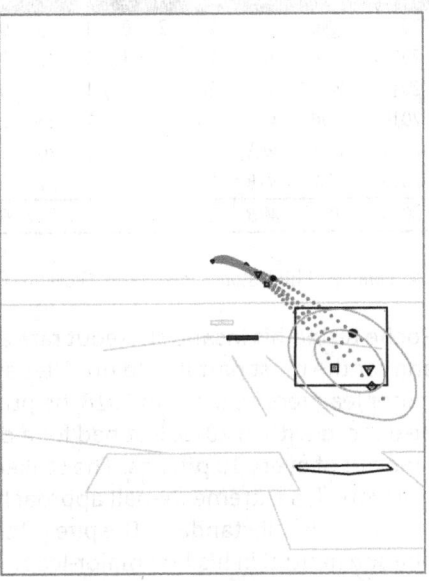

Type	Frequency	Velocity	H Movement	V Movement
● Fastball	30.0%	95.1 [108]	-11.7 [79]	-16.3 [99]
□ Sinker	18.9%	94.3 [109]	-16.1 [78]	-23.1 [90]
+ Cutter				
▲ Changeup				
✕ Splitter	3.2%	85.3 [101]	-17.3 [65]	-31.4 [93]
▽ Slider	9.3%	85.6 [105]	4 [96]	-32 [103]
◇ Curveball	37.3%	78.9 [101]	16.4 [136]	-48.4 [98]
⊕ Slow Curveball				
✱ Knuckleball				
▼ Screwball				

Colin Poche   LHP

Born: 01/17/94   Age: 26   Bats: L   Throws: L
Height: 6'3"   Weight: 235   Origin: Round 14, 2016 Draft (#419 overall)

YEAR	TEAM	LVL	AGE	W	L	SV	G	GS	IP	H	HR	BB/9	K/9	K	GB%	BABIP
2017	KNC	A	23	2	0	1	13	0	24²	16	0	2.2	16.1	44	40%	.372
2017	VIS	A+	23	1	1	2	18	0	25²	14	0	4.6	13.0	37	43%	.275
2018	WTN	AA	24	0	0	1	9	0	11	3	0	1.6	18.8	23	8%	.250
2018	DUR	AAA	24	5	0	1	28	2	50	29	2	3.1	14.0	78	28%	.297
2019	DUR	AAA	25	2	2	0	20	2	27¹	32	4	3.0	15.8	48	35%	.459
2019	TBA	MLB	25	5	5	2	51	0	51²	33	9	3.3	12.5	72	19%	.235
2020	TBA	MLB	26	3	3	0	54	0	58	42	9	3.3	12.2	78	24%	.267

Comparables: Phil Maton, James Pazos, Giovanny Gallegos

Poche tested his insane strikeout rate at the major-league level for the first time and for the most part it held up. After striking out just over 41 percent of the minor leaguers he faced in 2018, he punched out 35 percent of the big leaguers he danced with in 2019. Not bad for a dude that throws a 93-mph fastball nearly nine out of every 10 pitches. The strikeouts were good, but the location could use work; his extreme fly-ball approach means more homers when his command is substandard. Despite pitching with his left hand, Poche was platoon neutral in his first major-league run; a byproduct of not being reliant on a breaking pitch for outs. This will likely help him earn more high-leverage work in the future, especially if he can hone in on the location of his rising heater.

YEAR	TEAM	LVL	AGE	WHIP	ERA	DRA	WARP	MPH	FB%	WHF	CSP
2017	KNC	A	23	0.89	1.09	2.19	0.8				
2017	VIS	A+	23	1.05	1.40	2.23	0.8				
2018	WTN	AA	24	0.45	0.00	2.25	0.3				
2018	DUR	AAA	24	0.92	1.08	2.33	1.6				
2019	DUR	AAA	25	1.50	6.26	3.62	0.7				
2019	TBA	MLB	25	1.01	4.70	4.30	0.6	95.2	88.5	18.9	49.9
2020	TBA	MLB	26	1.10	3.07	3.42	1.1	94.8	90.1	19.2	50.8

Colin Poche, continued

	Pitch Shape vs LHH	Pitch Shape vs RHH
	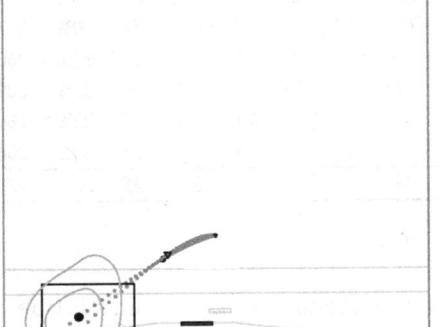	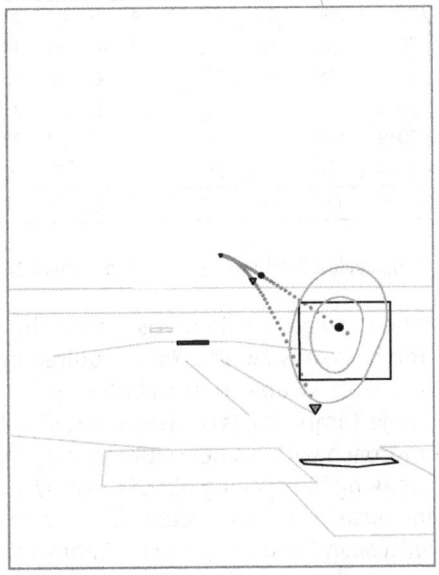

Type	Frequency	Velocity	H Movement	V Movement
● Fastball	88.5%	93.3 [103]	3.6 [114]	-9.8 [116]
☐ Sinker				
+ Cutter				
▲ Changeup				
✕ Splitter				
▽ Slider	10.1%	84.3 [99]	-7.2 [109]	-31.5 [105]
◇ Curveball				
⊕ Slow Curveball				
✳ Knuckleball				
▼ Screwball				

Trevor Richards RHP

Born: 05/15/93 Age: 27 Bats: R Throws: R
Height: 6'2" Weight: 190 Origin: Undrafted Free Agent, 2016

YEAR	TEAM	LVL	AGE	W	L	SV	G	GS	IP	H	HR	BB/9	K/9	K	GB%	BABIP
2017	JUP	A+	24	7	4	0	13	11	70^2	54	2	1.5	10.3	81	62%	.284
2017	JAX	AA	24	5	7	0	14	14	75^1	67	4	2.2	9.2	77	50%	.297
2018	NWO	AAA	25	3	2	0	6	6	39^1	31	4	0.9	8.5	37	50%	.260
2018	MIA	MLB	25	4	9	0	25	25	126^1	121	15	3.8	9.3	130	38%	.309
2019	MIA	MLB	26	3	12	0	23	20	112	104	16	4.1	8.3	103	38%	.286
2019	TBA	MLB	26	3	0	0	7	3	23^1	23	3	1.9	9.3	24	35%	.308
2020	TBA	MLB	27	3	2	0	33	3	48	43	7	3.3	8.5	45	38%	.278

Comparables: Brock Stewart, Domingo Germán, Mike Clevinger

When you google Richards' name, the first autocomplete is gray hair. It is true and he is only 26. The Rays acquired ol' pelo canoso at the trade deadline in an interstate swap with the Marlins. He was effective following the trade, but never made Tampa Bay's postseason roster. In a small sample size, he simplified his approach with his new club, leaning mostly on fastballs and changeups with breaking balls falling out of favor. The early returns were encouraging, with an increase in strikeout rate and a decrease in walks. Richards failed as a starter with Miami and there are too many talented arms ahead of him with the Rays to return to the rotation, but he also does not have the stuff that would allow him to dominate in short-relief, high-leverage situations. The bulk role that Tampa uses so effectively could be just what he needs to carve out a spot on the pitching staff going forward.

YEAR	TEAM	LVL	AGE	WHIP	ERA	DRA	WARP	MPH	FB%	WHF	CSP
2017	JUP	A+	24	0.93	2.17	2.90	1.9				
2017	JAX	AA	24	1.13	2.87	3.46	1.5				
2018	NWO	AAA	25	0.89	2.06	2.66	1.3				
2018	MIA	MLB	25	1.39	4.42	3.57	2.5	92.7	54.8	11.7	44.4
2019	MIA	MLB	26	1.38	4.50	5.69	0.1	92.8	42.3	12.8	45.9
2019	TBA	MLB	26	1.20	1.93	4.63	0.3	91.9	50	13	46.6
2020	TBA	MLB	27	1.27	3.98	4.22	0.6	92.2	49.1	12.5	45.9

Trevor Richards, continued

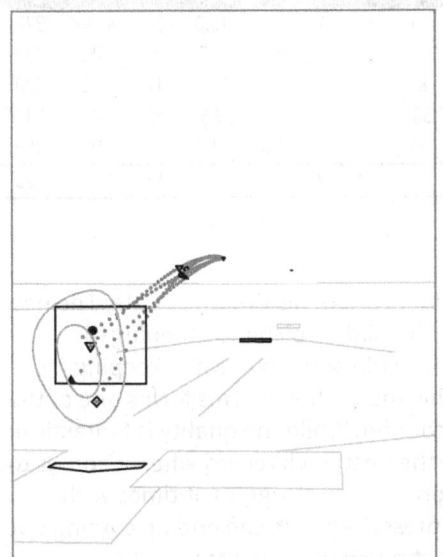
Pitch Shape vs LHH

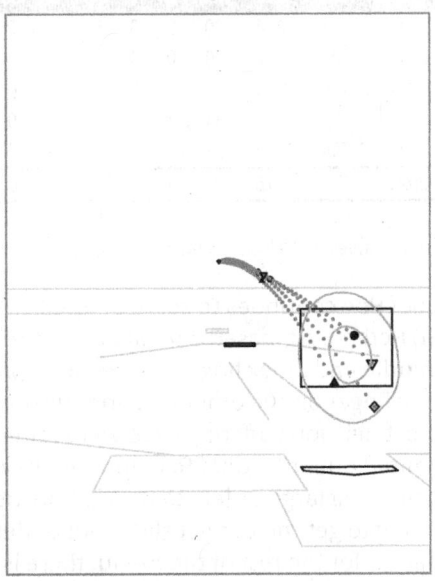
Pitch Shape vs RHH

Type	Frequency	Velocity	H Movement	V Movement
● Fastball	43.6%	91.3 [97]	-6.6 [101]	-13.6 [106]
☐ Sinker				
+ Cutter				
▲ Changeup	38.4%	83.8 [95]	-13.4 [89]	-27.5 [100]
✕ Splitter				
▽ Slider	10.5%	85.7 [105]	3.9 [96]	-28.6 [113]
◇ Curveball	7.5%	79.4 [103]	4 [86]	-45.3 [105]
✦ Slow Curveball				
✳ Knuckleball				
▼ Screwball				

Chaz Roe RHP

Born: 10/09/86 Age: 33 Bats: R Throws: R
Height: 6'5" Weight: 190 Origin: Round 1, 2005 Draft (#32 overall)

YEAR	TEAM	LVL	AGE	W	L	SV	G	GS	IP	H	HR	BB/9	K/9	K	GB%	BABIP
2017	DUR	AAA	30	0	3	4	17	0	21	18	1	2.1	15.0	35	43%	.370
2017	ATL	MLB	30	0	0	0	3	0	2	3	0	9.0	4.5	1	67%	.333
2017	TBA	MLB	30	0	0	0	9	0	8^2	4	1	3.1	12.5	12	50%	.200
2018	TBA	MLB	31	1	3	1	61	0	50^1	35	6	2.9	9.5	53	48%	.242
2019	TBA	MLB	32	1	3	1	71	0	51	49	3	5.5	11.5	65	44%	.359
2020	TBA	MLB	33	2	2	0	48	0	51	44	7	3.5	9.8	56	46%	.285

Comparables: Brad Brach, Sam Freeman, Luis García

Chef Roe continues to serve up quality sliders out of his Chez Roe Cafe. The now St. Petersburg-based culinary artist forms his sliders by hand. Keeping his middle and index fingers close, he grips one side of the ball while keeping his ring finger on the other end and tucking his thumb below. This forms one of the most delicious offerings you will ever encounter. While the quality is fantastic in limited quantity, Chef Roe does not have the best track record when it comes to delivering large orders to the right location. He also struggles at times with trying to get the perfect slider out under pressure which can end up coming out flat. As for the rest of the menu, there is not much to it. Unless you like meatballs, of course.

YEAR	TEAM	LVL	AGE	WHIP	ERA	DRA	WARP	MPH	FB%	WHF	CSP
2017	DUR	AAA	30	1.10	3.00	3.49	0.4				
2017	ATL	MLB	30	2.50	9.00	7.60	-0.1	95.1	53.3	6.7	54.1
2017	TBA	MLB	30	0.81	1.04	3.01	0.2	94.7	42.9	16.8	40.9
2018	TBA	MLB	31	1.01	3.58	3.71	0.7	94.5	47.4	11.7	49.4
2019	TBA	MLB	32	1.57	4.06	4.57	0.4	93.5	28.9	10.2	48.6
2020	TBA	MLB	33	1.26	3.84	4.07	0.6	93.0	36.4	10.8	47.3

Chaz Roe, continued

Pitch Shape vs LHH

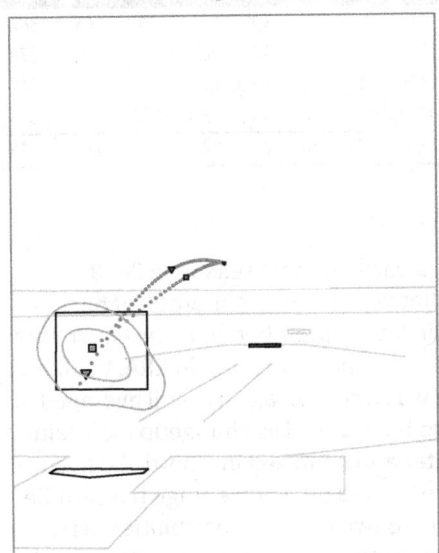

Pitch Shape vs RHH

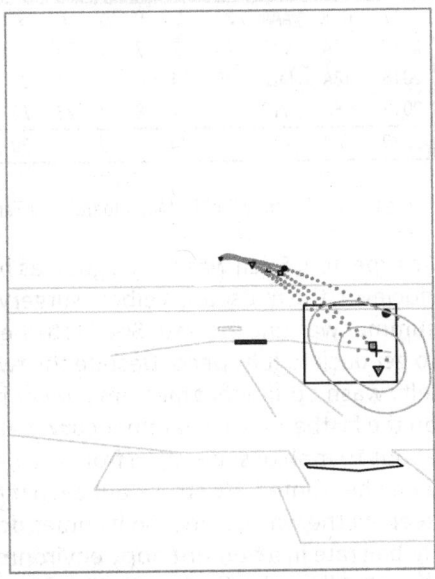

Type	Frequency	Velocity	H Movement	V Movement
● Fastball	6.4%	92.7 [101]	-5.2 [108]	-15.7 [101]
□ Sinker	22.5%	92.4 [99]	-11.5 [108]	-23.1 [91]
+ Cutter	6.5%	87.1 [90]	6.2 [126]	-26.9 [90]
▲ Changeup				
✕ Splitter				
▽ Slider	64.6%	81.3 [87]	20.1 [163]	-40.3 [79]
◇ Curveball				
⊕ Slow Curveball				
✱ Knuckleball				
▼ Screwball				

Blake Snell LHP

Born: 12/04/92   Age: 27   Bats: L   Throws: L
Height: 6'4"   Weight: 215   Origin: Round 1, 2011 Draft (#52 overall)

YEAR	TEAM	LVL	AGE	W	L	SV	G	GS	IP	H	HR	BB/9	K/9	K	GB%	BABIP
2017	DUR	AAA	24	5	0	0	7	7	44	43	5	3.1	12.5	61	46%	.362
2017	TBA	MLB	24	5	7	0	24	24	129^1	113	15	4.1	8.3	119	45%	.278
2018	TBA	MLB	25	21	5	0	31	31	180^2	112	16	3.2	11.0	221	46%	.241
2019	TBA	MLB	26	6	8	0	23	23	107	96	14	3.4	12.4	147	39%	.343
2020	TBA	MLB	27	10	8	0	28	28	154	125	18	4.1	12.8	220	41%	.315

Comparables: Anthony Banda, Matt Moore, Jake Faria

As expected, Snell was not as good as his award-winning season in 2018. However, the midseason elbow surgery that wiped out two months of his summer was unexpected. Snell returned in late September, but was never able to get back to full speed. Despite the two-and-a-half-run jump in ERA, the lanky lefty wasn't quite that far from pitcher he was a season ago. He still averaged 96 on the fastball with a hammer curveball to back it up. His changeup maintained about 10 mph of separation from the heater and he mixed in a hard slider/cutter when he wanted. He struck out even more batters on a percentage basis while keeping the walks static. So it comes down to two distinct possibilities: a rising fly-ball rate in a homer-happy environment or the weird goatee he attempted to pull off. All in all, a healthy Snell is one of the best pitchers in baseball. And with a team-friendly extension, he is also one of the most valuable pieces of a team built to win a lot over the next five seasons. Just don't tell him about trades while he's gaming.

YEAR	TEAM	LVL	AGE	WHIP	ERA	DRA	WARP	MPH	FB%	WHF	CSP
2017	DUR	AAA	24	1.32	2.66	3.78	0.9				
2017	TBA	MLB	24	1.33	4.04	4.05	2.2	96.5	55.1	11.4	40.4
2018	TBA	MLB	25	0.97	1.89	2.44	6.0	98.2	51.5	15.7	44.5
2019	TBA	MLB	26	1.27	4.29	3.59	2.5	97.6	48.4	18.1	42.8
2020	TBA	MLB	27	1.27	3.42	3.62	3.3	97.1	51.9	15.7	43.3

Blake Snell, continued

Pitch Shape vs LHH

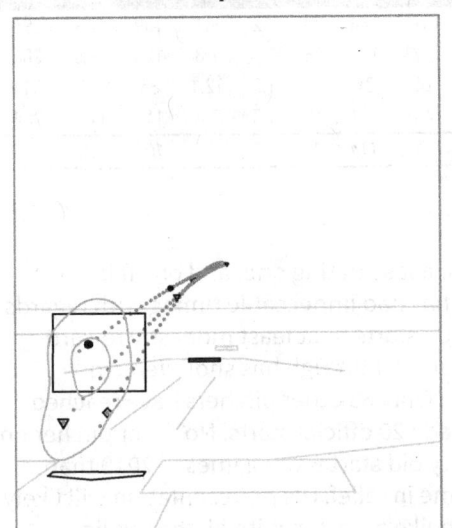

Pitch Shape vs RHH

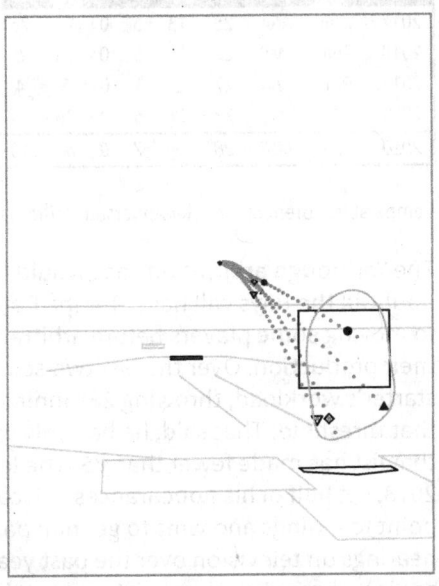

Type	Frequency	Velocity	H Movement	V Movement
● Fastball	48.4%	95.9 [110]	5.9 [104]	-10 [116]
□ Sinker				
+ Cutter				
▲ Changeup	20.4%	86.8 [105]	12 [96]	-23.2 [112]
✕ Splitter				
▽ Slider	6.8%	87.7 [114]	-4.2 [97]	-28 [115]
◇ Curveball	24.5%	81.4 [109]	-4.5 [88]	-44.4 [107]
✥ Slow Curveball				
✱ Knuckleball				
▼ Screwball				

Ryan Yarbrough LHP

Born: 12/31/91   Age: 28   Bats: R   Throws: L
Height: 6'5"   Weight: 210   Origin: Round 4, 2014 Draft (#111 overall)

YEAR	TEAM	LVL	AGE	W	L	SV	G	GS	IP	H	HR	BB/9	K/9	K	GB%	BABIP
2017	DUR	AAA	25	13	6	0	26	26	157^1	144	20	2.2	9.1	159	47%	.296
2018	TBA	MLB	26	16	6	0	38	6	147^1	140	18	3.1	7.8	128	39%	.288
2019	DUR	AAA	27	2	1	0	5	4	26	24	2	1.0	12.1	35	46%	.344
2019	TBA	MLB	27	11	6	0	28	14	141^2	121	15	1.3	7.4	117	44%	.264
2020	TBA	MLB	28	7	7	0	61	13	120	114	21	2.2	7.6	101	42%	.273

Comparables: Brent Suter, Tyler Anderson, Jarlin García

The Yarbrough arbitration case would be a fascinating one, and one it is doubtful the Rays will have. Tampa Bay has had impeccable timing with regards to moving some players before arbitration starts to at least modestly reward their production. Over the last two seasons, Yarbrough has shouldered a starter's workload, throwing 289 innings. Only 63 other pitchers have reached that threshold. That said, he has only made 20 official starts. No other pitcher on that list has made fewer than 35. The lefty did start more games in 2019 than 2018, yet half of his appearances still came in relief. His representation will likely point to innings and wins to get him paid like a starter. With all the public hearings on television over the past year, the one baseball fans would love to see is Yarbrough versus whatever employer he has at the time he is eligible.

YEAR	TEAM	LVL	AGE	WHIP	ERA	DRA	WARP	MPH	FB%	WHF	CSP
2017	DUR	AAA	25	1.16	3.43	4.46	2.1				
2018	TBA	MLB	26	1.29	3.91	4.82	0.3	91.7	63.9	10	50.6
2019	DUR	AAA	27	1.04	3.81	2.83	1.0				
2019	TBA	MLB	27	1.00	4.13	3.97	2.5	89.9	61	11	49.2
2020	TBA	MLB	28	1.19	4.00	4.36	1.4	90.2	62.7	10.6	50.2

Ryan Yarbrough, continued

Pitch Shape vs LHH

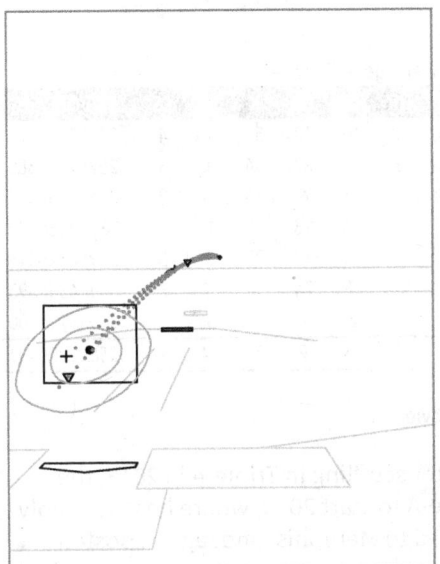

Pitch Shape vs RHH

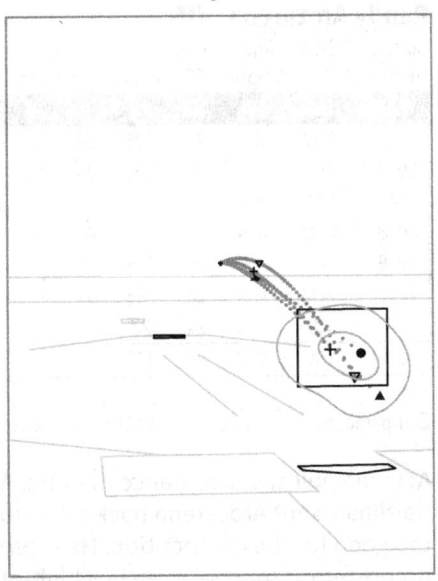

Type	Frequency	Velocity	H Movement	V Movement
● Fastball	24.1%	88.6 [89]	13 [73]	-21.7 [85]
☐ Sinker				
+ Cutter	36.9%	84.4 [73]	-1.4 [97]	-27.5 [87]
▲ Changeup	25.6%	79.9 [81]	15.6 [79]	-33.1 [83]
✕ Splitter				
▽ Slider	13.4%	73.2 [53]	-12.2 [130]	-44 [68]
◇ Curveball				
✦ Slow Curveball				
✱ Knuckleball				
▼ Screwball				

PLAYER COMMENTS WITHOUT GRAPHS

Randy Arozarena OF
Born: 02/28/95   Age: 25   Bats: R   Throws: R
Height: 5'11"   Weight: 170   Origin: International Free Agent, 2016

YEAR	TEAM	LVL	AGE	PA	R	2B	3B	HR	RBI	BB	K	SB	CS	AVG/OBP/SLG
2017	PMB	A+	22	295	38	22	3	8	40	13	53	10	4	.275/.333/.472
2017	SFD	AA	22	195	34	10	1	3	9	27	34	8	3	.252/.366/.380
2018	SFD	AA	23	102	22	5	0	7	21	6	25	9	3	.396/.455/.681
2018	MEM	AAA	23	311	42	16	0	5	28	28	59	17	5	.232/.328/.348
2019	SFD	AA	24	116	14	7	2	3	15	13	23	8	5	.309/.422/.515
2019	MEM	AAA	24	283	51	18	2	12	38	24	48	9	7	.358/.435/.593
2019	SLN	MLB	24	23	4	1	0	1	2	2	4	2	1	.300/.391/.500
2020	SLN	MLB	25	112	13	6	0	4	13	9	26	4	1	.258/.339/.431

Comparables: Jack Daniels, Jordan Luplow, Joe Lefebvre

At some point, performance matters. After scuffling in Triple-A in 2018, the Cardinals sent Arozarena back to Double-A to start 2019, where he was simply too good for the competition. He returned to Memphis, and, again, posted preposterous marks—even in a high-offense environment. Arozarena's lack of power has always held back his otherwise polished offensive game, yet as his standout season shows, the socialization of home runs can help players with a tweener profile emerge from the pack. Though he doesn't have the pedigree or major-league reps of other young Cardinals outfielders, it's hard to ignore his offensive track record and his defensive skills. In other words, there may be three a's in Arozarena, but we think he's a big-league player.

YEAR	TEAM	LVL	AGE	PA	DRC+	VORP	BABIP	BRR	FRAA	WARP
2017	PMB	A+	22	295	144	24.3	.313	-2.5	LF(47): 4.3, CF(13): -0.5	2.2
2017	SFD	AA	22	195	114	9.0	.299	2.7	LF(40): 0.1, CF(4): -0.9	0.9
2018	SFD	AA	23	102	200	15.4	.492	1.0	RF(12): 1.6, CF(6): -0.4	1.5
2018	MEM	AAA	23	311	83	9.3	.278	0.8	LF(49): -2.7, RF(18): 0.2	-0.1
2019	SFD	AA	24	116	160	10.9	.380	-0.5	CF(13): 0.9, LF(5): 0.0	0.9
2019	MEM	AAA	24	283	154	34.3	.404	-1.2	CF(25): -3.4, RF(20): 4.6	2.7
2019	SLN	MLB	24	23	84	0.3	.333	-1.7	RF(6): -0.1, CF(5): 0.5	-0.1
2020	SLN	MLB	25	112	110	4.9	.314	0.0	LF 0, CF 0	0.4

Vidal Brujan 2B

Born: 02/09/98 Age: 22 Bats: B Throws: R
Height: 5'9" Weight: 155 Origin: International Free Agent, 2014

YEAR	TEAM	LVL	AGE	PA	R	2B	3B	HR	RBI	BB	K	SB	CS	AVG/OBP/SLG
2017	HUD	A-	19	302	51	15	5	3	20	34	36	16	8	.285/.378/.415
2018	BGR	A	20	434	86	18	5	5	41	48	53	43	15	.313/.395/.427
2018	PCH	A+	20	114	26	7	2	4	12	15	15	12	4	.347/.434/.582
2019	PCH	A+	21	196	28	8	3	1	15	17	26	24	5	.290/.357/.386
2019	MNT	AA	21	233	28	9	4	3	25	20	35	24	8	.266/.336/.391
2020	TBA	MLB	22	35	3	2	0	1	3	3	6	1	1	.242/.305/.358

Comparables: Luis Valbuena, Corban Joseph, Thairo Estrada

In a system full of second-base prospects, Brujan stands out for multiple reasons. A switch-hitter signed for less than a waiver claim in 2014, he has easy plus speed and a plus hit tool that makes him an ideal candidate to top a lineup for a decade. His contact and plate discipline skills border on elite, and for his minor-league career he's struck out only 10 more times than he's walked. Brujan ended the 2019 season in Double-A and after a strong Arizona Fall League stint will be knocking on the door of the majors in 2020. The biggest question for the 22-year-old is where he'll end up defensively. He mostly mans the keystone not because of a lack of skill that would move him off short, but due to Willy Adames being ahead of him on the depth chart and Wander Franco peeking over his shoulder.

YEAR	TEAM	LVL	AGE	PA	DRC+	VORP	BABIP	BRR	FRAA	WARP
2017	HUD	A-	19	302	155	20.4	.321	-3.7	2B(65): 14.9	3.4
2018	BGR	A	20	434	144	41.0	.351	8.2	2B(88): 4.4	4.6
2018	PCH	A+	20	114	172	13.8	.380	1.0	2B(24): 4.5	1.7
2019	PCH	A+	21	196	131	18.2	.333	5.5	2B(29): 0.7, SS(14): 0.7	2.0
2019	MNT	AA	21	233	95	4.8	.304	-2.6	2B(33): 2.7, SS(14): -0.1	0.6
2020	TBA	MLB	22	35	80	0.5	.284	0.0	2B 1	0.1

Xavier Edwards SS

Born: 08/09/99   Age: 20   Bats: B   Throws: R
Height: 5'10"   Weight: 175   Origin: Round 1, 2018 Draft (#38 overall)

YEAR	TEAM	LVL	AGE	PA	R	2B	3B	HR	RBI	BB	K	SB	CS	AVG/OBP/SLG
2018	PDR	RK	18	88	19	4	1	0	11	13	10	12	1	.384/.471/.466
2018	TRI	A-	18	107	21	4	0	0	5	18	15	10	0	.314/.438/.360
2019	FTW	A	19	344	44	13	4	1	30	30	35	20	9	.336/.392/.414
2019	LEL	A+	19	217	32	5	4	0	13	14	19	14	2	.301/.349/.367
2020	TBA	MLB	20	251	24	11	1	2	22	21	38	10	2	.278/.341/.367

Comparables: José Ramírez, J.P. Crawford, Victor Robles

His full season debut couldn't have gone much better. Edwards flashed the speed and contact skills of an old-school switch-hitting table-setter and enough athleticism and arm strength to augur a future at shortstop that is more than a pipedream, with second base and center field listed as his safety schools. Edwards rarely swings and misses, sprays the ball to all fields and uses his wheels to beat out slow rollers and turn doubles into triples. His frame and swing aren't built for power, but Edwards isn't a slap-hitter. Instead, he plays within himself and doesn't sell out, focusing on putting the ball in play, reaching base and being an all-around pest once he gets there. Given his ability to avoid outs, produce runs with his legs and provide solid glovework at a premium defensive position, it's easy to dream on Edwards growing into the X-factor atop a big-league lineup.

YEAR	TEAM	LVL	AGE	PA	DRC+	VORP	BABIP	BRR	FRAA	WARP
2018	PDR	RK	18	88	187	13.5	.438	1.9	SS(15): 3.1	1.5
2018	TRI	A-	18	107	181	9.9	.380	-0.3	SS(19): -1.1, 2B(5): 0.0	1.1
2019	FTW	A	19	344	141	24.6	.371	0.2	2B(51): 4.1, SS(21): 3.1	3.4
2019	LEL	A+	19	217	102	15.3	.331	3.5	2B(35): 0.2, SS(9): -1.2	0.9
2020	TBA	MLB	20	251	92	6.1	.325	0.6	2B 2, SS 0	0.8

Wander Franco SS

Born: 03/01/01 Age: 19 Bats: B Throws: R
Height: 5'10" Weight: 189 Origin: International Free Agent, 2017

YEAR	TEAM	LVL	AGE	PA	R	2B	3B	HR	RBI	BB	K	SB	CS	AVG/OBP/SLG
2018	PRI	RK	17	273	46	10	7	11	57	27	19	4	3	.351/.418/.587
2019	BGR	A	18	272	42	16	5	6	29	30	20	14	9	.318/.390/.506
2019	PCH	A+	18	223	40	11	2	3	24	26	15	4	5	.339/.408/.464
2020	TBA	MLB	19	251	27	12	2	5	27	25	31	2	1	.271/.348/.412

Comparables: Vladimir Guerrero Jr., Mike Trout, Manny Machado

Welcome to the 2020 Baseball Prospectus Annual, where Franco is rated as the top prospect in baseball. Despite being extremely young for his level, the teenager posted the third-highest DRC+ in the Florida State League while making dazzling plays in the field as a shortstop. He has a plus-plus hit tool from both sides with power that is already showing in games from the left—30 of his 36 extra-base hits came when facing right-handers. He can run. He can throw. He can play either shortstop or second base, though there's no reason to move him off the former yet. He is a superstar in waiting.

    While we are here, let's just get next year's comment out of the way too. Welcome to the 2021 Baseball Prospectus Annual, where Franco is rated as the top prospect in baseball. Despite being young for his level, the teenager posted elite statistics while making dazzling plays in the field as a shortstop. He has a plus hit-tool from either side, and his power is already showing in games from the left. He can run. He can throw. He can play either shortstop or second base, though there's no reason to move him off the former yet. He is a superstar in waiting.

YEAR	TEAM	LVL	AGE	PA	DRC+	VORP	BABIP	BRR	FRAA	WARP
2018	PRI	RK	17	273	166	35.4	.346	-0.4	SS(53): -5.3	2.4
2019	BGR	A	18	272	158	29.3	.318	0.1	SS(53): -1.0	2.6
2019	PCH	A+	18	223	175	30.9	.346	4.3	SS(44): 8.1	3.9
2020	TBA	MLB	19	251	106	10.0	.294	-0.3	SS 2	1.3

Ronaldo Hernandez   C

Born: 11/11/97   Age: 22   Bats: R   Throws: R
Height: 6'1"   Weight: 185   Origin: International Free Agent, 2014

YEAR	TEAM	LVL	AGE	PA	R	2B	3B	HR	RBI	BB	K	SB	CS	AVG/OBP/SLG
2017	PRI	RK	19	246	42	22	1	5	40	16	39	2	2	.332/.382/.507
2018	BGR	A	20	449	68	20	1	21	79	31	69	10	4	.284/.339/.494
2019	PCH	A+	21	427	43	19	3	9	60	17	65	7	0	.265/.299/.397
2020	TBA	MLB	22	35	4	2	0	1	4	2	7	0	0	.254/.300/.435

Comparables: Meibrys Viloria, Abiatal Avelino, Dom Nuñez

A converted infielder out of Colombia, Hernandez continues to climb the organizational ladder as a catcher. He was named to the Futures Game in July and ended the season having provided a slightly above-average offensive performance. His raw power was a bit stifled in the humid air of the Florida State League, and he really would prefer not to walk, but his average bat combined with his plus arm makes him a potential starter at catcher. At present, there's no one in the depth chart that should stand in the way of him getting a shot at some point over the next two seasons.

YEAR	TEAM	LVL	AGE	PA	DRC+	VORP	BABIP	BRR	FRAA	WARP
2017	PRI	RK	19	246	150	24.4	.379	2.5	C(43): 1.1	2.6
2018	BGR	A	20	449	136	39.2	.292	-0.8	C(85): 1.2	3.5
2019	PCH	A+	21	427	105	20.3	.290	1.8	C(81): 1.9	2.3
2020	TBA	MLB	22	35	94	1.3	.290	-0.1	C 0	0.1

Greg Jones SS

Born: 03/07/98 Age: 22 Bats: B Throws: R
Height: 6'2" Weight: 175 Origin: Round 1, 2019 Draft (#22 overall)

YEAR	TEAM	LVL	AGE	PA	R	2B	3B	HR	RBI	BB	K	SB	CS	AVG/OBP/SLG
2019	HUD	A-	21	218	39	13	4	1	24	22	56	19	8	.335/.413/.461
2020	TBA	MLB	22	251	22	12	1	4	23	16	84	3	1	.239/.295/.348

Comparables: Mark Hamilton, J.D. Martinez, Alex Dickerson

The first player to ever be selected in the first round out of UNC-Wilmington, Jones saw his stock rise after a tremendous sophomore year. The shortstop can flat out fly. It is easy, 80-grade speed that will help keep him in the middle of the diamond. Jones might play the six in his current state, but some evaluators see his ultimate home in center field where his best tool can be put on display more regularly. A switch-hitter with pop from both sides, Jones still has to answer questions about his hit tool from both sides of the dish. This was evident in his pro debut at Hudson Valley, where despite good results, he struck out in a quarter of his plate appearances. Don't be surprised if the Rays are more aggressive with him than usual with assignments, as Jones will turn 22 before Opening Day.

YEAR	TEAM	LVL	AGE	PA	DRC+	VORP	BABIP	BRR	FRAA	WARP
2019	HUD	A-	21	218	174	25.2	.467	4.2	SS(21): 2.2	2.6
2020	TBA	MLB	22	251	73	-0.9	.358	0.0	SS 1	0.0

Brendan McKay   LHP

Born: 12/18/95   Age: 24   Bats: L   Throws: L
Height: 6'2"   Weight: 212   Origin: Round 1, 2017 Draft (#4 overall)

YEAR	TEAM	LVL	AGE	PA	R	2B	3B	HR	RBI	BB	K	SB	CS	AVG/OBP/SLG
2017	HUD	A-	21	149	16	4	1	4	22	21	33	2	0	.232/.349/.376
2018	BGR	A	22	91	12	2	0	1	16	28	13	0	0	.254/.484/.333
2018	PCH	A+	22	139	19	6	1	5	21	16	38	0	0	.210/.317/.403
2019	MNT	AA	23	90	8	2	0	0	8	7	27	0	1	.167/.256/.192
2019	DUR	AAA	23	78	11	2	0	5	11	10	24	1	0	.239/.346/.493
2019	TBA	MLB	23	11	2	0	0	1	1	1	2	0	0	.200/.273/.500
2020	TBA	MLB	24	35	3	1	0	1	4	4	11	0	0	.206/.297/.349

Comparables: Chris McGuiness, Chris Shaw, Pete Alonso

The Shohei Ohtani comps can stop for now as the Rays will have to settle for McKay just being a really good left-handed starter instead of a two-headed dragon. The Rays took away McKay's first base glove to start the season and then his bat somewhere along the way. He still may make the occasional start at designated hitter—and even with a 26-man roster, it will still be valuable to have a pitcher that can also hit a little—but McKay's on his way towards leaving that double life behind. He was nearly unhittable to start his career before the league caught up to him. By the end of the year, concerns about workload took over and he didn't throw over 65 pitches in an appearance after mid-August. Despite the ups and downs, McKay showed stuff and poise that makes him a potential number two or three starter. He has a four-pitch mix led by a low-to-mid 90s fastball and a true, plus curveball. Developing command led to some home run issues at the highest level, but he has the ability to repeat and turn that into a strength. The Rays may play some games early in the year with regards to service time and innings totals, but McKay should toss his most important pitches for Tampa Bay in 2020.

YEAR	TEAM	LVL	AGE	PA	DRC+	VORP	BABIP	BRR	FRAA	WARP
2017	HUD	A-	21	149	120	3.7	.281	-1.3	1B(21): -1.1, P(6): 0.1	0.2
2018	BGR	A	22	91	180	1.0	.306	-3.1	1B(9): -0.3, P(6): 0.1	0.5
2018	PCH	A+	22	139	97	1.5	.260	0.5	1B(18): -0.4, P(11): -0.3	0.1
2019	MNT	AA	23	90	50	-4.2	.245	0.3	P(8): 0.5	-0.3
2019	DUR	AAA	23	78	94	1.3	.289	-0.3	P(7): -0.2	0.0
2019	TBA	MLB	23	11	57	0.2	.143	-0.1	P(13): -0.1	0.0
2020	TBA	MLB	24	35	77	-1.2	.288	0.0	1B 0	-0.1

Yoshitomo Tsutsugoh   3B/OF
Born: 11/26/91   Age: 28   Bats: L   Throws: R
Height: 6'0"   Weight: 210   Origin: International Free Agent, 2019

Every player in NPB has a cheer the crowd sings as they step up to the plate. "High into the Yokohama sky, hit a home run, Tsutsugo," were the first words of the Rays' newest import. (The Trop crowd might want to alter the lyrics to "hit the C-ring.") Predictably, Tsutsugo has impressive raw power, having wallopped 185 home runs over his last six seasons in Japan, including 44 in 2016. He isn't a one-dimensional, pull-happy slugger, however. He'll take his fair share of walks, and he's willing to spray liners to all fields. Defensively, he's passable in left field (and has some history at third base), but an optimal deployment has him at DH. Tsutsugo is an especially rare surname in Japan, and the Rays hope his production proves as special.

Anthony Banda LHP

Born: 08/10/93 Age: 26 Bats: L Throws: L
Height: 6'2" Weight: 225 Origin: Round 10, 2012 Draft (#335 overall)

YEAR	TEAM	LVL	AGE	W	L	SV	G	GS	IP	H	HR	BB/9	K/9	K	GB%	BABIP
2017	RNO	AAA	23	8	7	0	22	22	122	125	15	3.8	8.6	116	43%	.317
2017	ARI	MLB	23	2	3	0	8	4	25^2	26	1	3.5	8.8	25	39%	.329
2018	DUR	AAA	24	4	3	0	8	8	42	43	3	3.9	10.5	49	40%	.360
2018	TBA	MLB	24	1	0	0	3	1	14^2	12	1	1.8	6.1	10	49%	.262
2019	DUR	AAA	25	2	3	0	9	4	28^1	28	7	3.5	8.6	27	41%	.284
2019	TBA	MLB	25	0	0	0	3	0	4	6	0	0.0	4.5	2	25%	.375
2020	TBA	MLB	26	1	1	0	3	3	13	15	3	3.4	6.3	9	39%	.298

Comparables: Jake Faria, Blake Snell, Dana Eveland

Acquired in 2018 in a trade with the Arizona Diamondbacks for Steven Souza, Banda has similarly struggled to stay on the field. After missing much of the last two seasons due to Tommy John surgery, the lefty returned to the mound but did little at the big-league level. He spent about six weeks in a hybrid starter/bulk guy role at Triple-A Durham before making a couple of mop-up appearances in Tampa Bay. That said, making it all the way back from injury is probably sufficient progress enough—though it's not ideal that he showed diminished velocity upon his return in relief. Banda still throws in the low-90s and can scrape higher with an above-average changeup and a sparingly-used slider. On the surface, Banda would fit nicely in a Jalen Beeks or Ryan Yarbrough type role, but he'll need to miss more bats to do so.

YEAR	TEAM	LVL	AGE	WHIP	ERA	DRA	WARP	MPH	FB%	WHF	CSP
2017	RNO	AAA	23	1.44	5.39	4.15	2.1				
2017	ARI	MLB	23	1.40	5.96	4.21	0.4	96.7	63.4	11.7	45.1
2018	DUR	AAA	24	1.45	3.64	5.21	0.2				
2018	TBA	MLB	24	1.02	3.68	4.75	0.1	96.6	77.8	10.6	57
2019	DUR	AAA	25	1.38	6.04	4.75	0.5				
2019	TBA	MLB	25	1.50	6.75	5.51	0.0	94.3	55.9	3.4	54.8
2020	TBA	MLB	26	1.52	6.02	5.89	0.0	96.0	68.4	10.5	54.1

Shane Baz RHP

Born: 06/17/99 Age: 21 Bats: R Throws: R
Height: 6'2" Weight: 190 Origin: Round 1, 2017 Draft (#12 overall)

YEAR	TEAM	LVL	AGE	W	L	SV	G	GS	IP	H	HR	BB/9	K/9	K	GB%	BABIP
2017	PIR	RK	18	0	3	0	10	10	23²	26	2	5.3	7.2	19	51%	.348
2018	BRI	RK	19	4	3	0	10	10	45¹	45	2	4.6	10.7	54	64%	.344
2018	PRI	RK	19	0	2	0	2	2	7	11	1	7.7	6.4	5	48%	.417
2019	BGR	A	20	3	2	0	17	17	81¹	63	5	4.1	9.6	87	39%	.279
2020	TBA	MLB	21	2	2	0	33	0	35	35	6	4.0	7.8	30	37%	.294

Comparables: Drew Anderson, Elvin Ramirez, Yennsy Diaz

With Austin Meadows' hitting and Tyler Glasnow's pitching, the Rays have already won the Chris Archer trade. Baz is just rubbing salt in the wound. The PTBNL in the mid-summer 2018 swap has the ability, and now the on-field production, to make this transaction one of the most lopsided moves of the decade. In his first full-season assignment, he struck out more than a batter per inning while keeping the ball in the yard. He struggled with control—let's not talk command yet—but that is a known issue and one that will ultimately define his ceiling. As is, he can reach the upper-90s with his fastball and has a pair of breaking balls that flash plus ability. Even his change projects to average and he has some room to fill out his naturally athletic frame. If he can clean up his delivery a bit to harness more of that command, Baz could be a dark horse for the top pitching prospect in baseball by the end of 2020.

YEAR	TEAM	LVL	AGE	WHIP	ERA	DRA	WARP	MPH	FB%	WHF	CSP
2017	PIR	RK	18	1.69	3.80	7.48	-0.4				
2018	BRI	RK	19	1.50	3.97	6.79	-0.3				
2018	PRI	RK	19	2.43	7.71	7.16	-0.1				
2019	BGR	A	20	1.23	2.99	3.88	1.2				
2020	TBA	MLB	21	1.45	4.97	5.00	0.1				

Brent Honeywell Jr. RHP
Born: 03/31/95   Age: 25   Bats: R   Throws: R
Height: 6'2"   Weight: 180   Origin: Round 2, 2014 Draft (#72 overall)

YEAR	TEAM	LVL	AGE	W	L	SV	G	GS	IP	H	HR	BB/9	K/9	K	GB%	BABIP
2017	MNT	AA	22	1	1	0	2	2	13	4	1	2.8	13.8	20	45%	.158
2017	DUR	AAA	22	12	8	0	24	24	123^2	130	11	2.3	11.1	152	42%	.366
2020	TBA	MLB	25	3	3	0	29	5	47	46	7	3.2	9.5	50	38%	.308

Comparables: Mitch Keller, Zack Littell, Stephen Gonsalves

Honeywell missed all of 2018 after undergoing Tommy John surgery. He was poised to make a mid-season debut in 2019 until he experienced a few minor setbacks and then a major one. The prized right-hander fractured his right elbow and has now gone two seasons without throwing a competitive pitch. Once again, the Rays are hoping for a mid-year return, but instead of the 23-year-old starter they thought they had in 2018, he will be a 25-year-old with more battlescars than pitches thrown at the major-league level. Honeywell has always been more of a pitcher than a thrower, so even with the arm ailments, he possesses the ceiling of an above-average starter because of his control, five-pitch mix and feel for the craft.

YEAR	TEAM	LVL	AGE	WHIP	ERA	DRA	WARP	MPH	FB%	WHF	CSP
2017	MNT	AA	22	0.62	2.08	1.98	0.5				
2017	DUR	AAA	22	1.30	3.64	4.26	2.0				
2020	TBA	MLB	25	1.34	4.32	4.53	0.4				

Shane McClanahan   LHP

Born: 04/28/97   Age: 23   Bats: L   Throws: L
Height: 6'1"   Weight: 200   Origin: Round 1C, 2018 Draft (#31 overall)

YEAR	TEAM	LVL	AGE	W	L	SV	G	GS	IP	H	HR	BB/9	K/9	K	GB%	BABIP
2019	BGR	A	22	4	4	0	11	10	53	38	3	5.3	12.6	74	48%	.304
2019	PCH	A+	22	6	1	0	9	8	49^1	33	1	1.5	10.8	59	44%	.250
2019	MNT	AA	22	1	1	0	4	4	18^1	30	3	2.9	10.3	21	43%	.450
2020	TBA	MLB	23	2	2	0	33	0	35	34	5	3.4	9.4	37	41%	.308

Comparables: Greg Smith, Gregory Soto, Steven Matz

Having already drafted arguably the best prep lefty pitcher in the 2018 draft, Matthew Liberatore, the Rays were ecstatic to see one of the best college southpaws—certainly the best in their backyard —sitting there for them with the 31st overall pick. The junior from the University of South Florida impressed during his first full-year in pro ball, making the wide trek from Bowling Green to Montgomery in a single season. In between his starting and ending point, he turned home briefly to dominate the Florida State League with nearly eight strikeouts versus every walk. He lives in the mid-90s with the strength to ramp up if needed. His changeup projects to be above-average and his curve is already there. There is some concern about his delivery, which is only heightened by the fact he already has Tommy John on his resume. The upside is a middle-of-the-rotation lefty. The Rays should let him continue on that path but find comfort in knowing they could turn him loose as a late-inning reliever at any time.

YEAR	TEAM	LVL	AGE	WHIP	ERA	DRA	WARP	MPH	FB%	WHF	CSP
2019	BGR	A	22	1.30	3.40	3.83	0.8				
2019	PCH	A+	22	0.83	1.46	2.48	1.5				
2019	MNT	AA	22	1.96	8.35	7.93	-0.7				
2020	TBA	MLB	23	1.36	4.37	4.48	0.3				

Tampa Bay Rays 2020

LINEOUTS

Hitters

HITTER	POS	TEAM	LVL	AGE	PA	R	2B	3B	HR	RBI	BB	K	SB	CS	AVG/OBP/SLG	DRC+	WARP
Roberto Alvarez	C	BGR	A	19	406	30	13	3	3	42	17	70	2	0	.249/.291/.324	74	-0.3
Emilio Bonifacio	UT	DUR	AAA	34	288	48	19	3	8	36	25	63	15	6	.286/.353/.475	102	1.1
Dylan Cozens	OF	PHI	MLB	25	1	0	0	0	0	0	0	0	0	0	.000/.000/.000	82	0.0
	OF	LEH	AAA	25	99	20	1	2	6	15	20	42	5	2	.167/.333/.462	96	0.6
Johnny Davis	OF	TBA	MLB	29	4	5	0	1	0	0	0	2	0	0	.250/.250/.750	69	0.0
Lucius Fox	MI	DUR	AAA	21	49	6	0	1	0	1	6	15	2	0	.143/.250/.190	47	0.0
	MI	MNT	AA	21	431	60	16	8	3	33	53	89	37	11	.230/.340/.342	106	2.0
Niko Hulsizer	OF	GRL	A	22	256	46	17	1	15	49	37	75	4	1	.268/.395/.574	186	2.9
	OF	RCU	A+	22	98	15	6	0	5	18	9	33	3	2	.259/.327/.506	100	0.5
	OF	PCH	A+	22	39	4	2	0	1	4	4	11	0	1	.235/.308/.382	96	0.1
Josh Lowe	OF	MNT	AA	21	519	70	23	4	18	62	59	132	30	9	.252/.341/.442	128	3.3
Brian O'Grady	1B	CIN	MLB	27	48	4	2	1	2	3	4	17	0	0	.190/.292/.429	76	-0.1
	1B	LOU	AAA	27	489	71	30	1	28	77	51	136	20	4	.280/.359/.550	111	1.8
Kevin Padlo	INF	MNT	AA	22	277	39	20	0	12	35	47	70	11	4	.250/.383/.505	167	3.5
	INF	DUR	AAA	22	155	25	11	1	9	27	21	46	1	0	.290/.400/.595	128	1.3
Michael Perez	C	DUR	AAA	26	216	23	7	0	13	42	28	51	0	2	.245/.338/.495	116	1.5
	C	TBA	MLB	26	55	6	5	0	0	2	8	19	0	0	.217/.345/.326	74	0.1
Garrett Whitley	OF	PCH	A+	22	439	51	25	7	10	40	62	163	16	12	.226/.339/.412	119	1.1

One of these days, a catching prospect will work out for Tampa Bay. **Roberto Alvarez** is trying to be that one. ⓧ If **Emilio Bonifácio**'s rate stats on the diamond were anything like his confirmed 30-percent restaurant tipping practices, he'd have spent his season leaving gratuities in Tampa, Chicago and New York instead of Durham, Charlotte and Syracuse. ⓧ The Rays are paying **Dylan Cozens** to rehab from a foot injury. Meanwhile, the Buffalo Sabres selected him seventh overall in the 2019 NHL draft. ⓧ **Johnny Davis** came out of nowhere—well the Mexican League actually—to score some of the Rays' most important runs in September as a designated runner. ⓧ **Lucius Fox** will need to start hitting fast otherwise he will become lost in an ever-expanding middle infield depth chart. ⓧ Long-hair, don't care. **Niko Hulsizer** has the chance to be a solid hitting outfielder in the majors one day. ⓧ **Josh Lowe** is a former first-round pick with a lot of tools, and has a brother that raps with Ji-Man Choi. ⓧ **Brian O'Grady** is a 27-year-old who finally got a full look at Triple-A. To his credit, he hit just fine there; alas, it's hard to imagine him making enough contact in the majors to be more than an up-and-down guy—even if the power *is* legit. ⓧ After scuffling in the low minors over the last two years, **Kevin Padlo** hit the ol' UPGRADE button in Double-A and Triple-A, and now sits on the doorstep of the majors in 2020. ⓧ **Michael Perez** has some offensive chops, which is more than most catchers can say. He just needs an extended look to see how sharp his chops really are. ⓧ Ciara is married to Russell Wilson and has a child with rapper Future. **Garrett Whitley** currently looks like what you would get if Russell Wilson and Future had a child of their own. That is about the nicest thing you can say about this former first-round pick.

Pitchers

PITCHER	TEAM	LVL	AGE	W	L	SV	G	GS	IP	H	HR	BB/9	K/9	K	GB%	WHIP	ERA	DRA	WARP
John Doxakis	HUD	A-	20	0	0	0	12	10	32^2	20	0	3.0	8.5	31	51%	0.95	1.93	3.07	0.8
Peter Fairbanks	DEB	A+	25	1	0	2	11	0	12^1	10	0	2.9	10.9	15	59%	1.14	2.92	3.64	0.2
	FRI	AA	25	1	0	0	6	0	7^1	2	0	0.0	17.2	14	70%	0.27	0.00	1.71	0.3
	NAS	AAA	25	0	0	0	7	0	6^1	10	1	2.8	15.6	11	33%	1.89	11.37	3.66	0.2
	DUR	AAA	25	1	2	0	16	1	17^2	15	3	3.1	15.3	30	44%	1.19	5.09	2.49	0.6
	TBA	MLB	25	2	1	2	13	0	12^1	17	1	2.2	9.5	13	43%	1.62	5.11	4.77	0.1
	TEX	MLB	25	0	2	0	8	0	8^2	8	4	7.3	15.6	15	42%	1.73	9.35	3.79	0.1
J.J. Goss	RAY	Rk	18	1	3	0	9	8	17	19	1	1.1	8.5	16	46%	1.24	5.82	4.59	0.3
Seth Johnson	RAY	Rk	20	0	0	0	5	5	10	7	0	1.8	6.3	7	43%	0.90	0.00	2.02	0.4
	PRI	Rk+	20	0	1	0	4	4	7	10	0	1.3	11.6	9	40%	1.57	5.14	6.47	0.0
Hoby Milner	DUR	AAA	28	3	3	12	50	0	61^2	47	7	1.9	13.0	89	44%	0.97	3.06	1.86	2.6
	TBA	MLB	28	0	0	0	4	0	3^2	4	0	2.5	7.4	3	25%	1.36	7.36	5.33	0.0
Joe Ryan	BGR	A	23	2	2	0	6	6	27^2	19	2	3.6	15.3	47	29%	1.08	2.93	2.91	0.7
	PCH	A+	23	7	2	0	15	13	82^2	47	3	1.3	12.2	112	38%	0.71	1.42	2.02	3.0
	MNT	AA	23	0	0	0	3	3	13^1	11	2	2.7	16.2	24	27%	1.12	3.38	4.14	0.1
Phoenix Sanders	MNT	AA	24	3	3	15	37	1	49^2	35	3	4.2	10.3	57	47%	1.17	1.81	3.84	0.5
	DUR	AAA	24	1	0	0	8	0	11^1	9	2	2.4	8.7	11	42%	1.06	2.38	2.86	0.4
Aaron Slegers	DUR	AAA	26	6	7	0	26	15	112^1	130	22	2.2	6.4	80	43%	1.41	5.05	5.42	1.2
	TBA	MLB	26	0	0	1	1	0	3	3	1	0.0	0.0	0	36%	1.00	3.00	6.73	0.0

A second-round pick from Texas A&M, J to the Muah a.k.a. **John Doxakis** could be a mid-rotation lefty with more finesse than stuff or a reliever with more stuff than finesse. ⓧ **Peter Fairbanks** throws really hard toward a general area. Sometimes it works. Sometimes it doesn't. ⓧ The 36th selection in the 2019 draft, **J.J. Goss** is a projectable righty from Texas with a potential three-pitch mix and control. ⓧ **Seth Johnson** was a hitter in JUCO, but became a day-one draft pick as a pitcher who can throw in the upper-90s with two potential bat-missing secondaries. ⓧ After the war, Lt. **Hoby Milner** retired to the Tampa Bay area where he was diagnosed with a cervical nerve issue. ⓧ You know that meme where the cat looks into the mirror and sees a lion? That is **Joe Ryan**, the Rays' minor-league pitcher of the year. ⓧ **Phoenix Sanders** is a useful relief prospect from Augsburg, Germany and of the five players the Rays took out of the Tampa-based University of South Florida last decade, he's likely to make the majors first.

Tampa Bay Rays 2020

⚾ Here's a fun fact. Did you know **Aaron Slegers** is really tall? Oh, we said that for the last three years? Well, he still is. Check back next year for an update.

Rays Prospects

The State of the System
It's not quite as deep or quite as good as last year's version, but the Rays still have an extremely strong system topped by the best prospect in baseball.

The Top Ten

──────── ★ ★ ★ *2020 Top 101 Prospect* **#1** ★ ★ ★ ────────

1
Wander Franco SS   OFP: 70   ETA: 2021
Born: 03/01/01   Age: 19   Bats: B   Throws: R   Height: 5'10"   Weight: 189
Origin: International Free Agent, 2017

The Report: The Rays signed Franco for nearly $4 million back in 2017, and that is going to end up looking like a bargain. "El Patrón" was the best hitter in both the Midwest and Florida State League this year, putting up excellent numbers against much older competition. The bat is elite, reminiscent of Vlad Jr., a rare combination of contact and power. Blessed with a superb eye and plus bat speed, Franco commands the zone, gladly taking walks, but also punishing mistakes. This summer at Bowling Green the unparalleled bat control was on display as Franco went nearly two weeks without a swing and miss. The raw power is plus and will play plus in-game as he continues to mature physically.

The rest of the tools are not nearly as sexy. Lacking the arm strength for short, he'll eventually find a home at second base where he will be an above-average defender. On the bases, he's extremely aggressive to the point of recklessness, at times, but with continued experience he should become an average baserunner. Neither of these limitations should be much of a concern with a bat that looks to eventually become one of the best in the league.

Variance: Medium. Inherent risk due to the fact that he's still a teenager and yet to play above High-A but watch him hit and your worries will be put to rest.

Mark Barry's Fantasy Take: It's hard to read Franco's write up and not get Tex Avery vibes (no, I didn't have to google that as opposed to just writing "the wolf cartoon with the bulging eyes"). The home run numbers don't look great, but the slugging numbers sure do, and there's plenty of time for that raw power to manifest itself in the form of dingers. Even Franco's limitations (might move to second base) don't really matter in a fantasy context, so there really aren't any nits to pick here. Last season, Nostra-Carsley predicted that Franco "could rank 1-1 a year from now". Turns out he knows some stuff some of the time. The 18-year-old is a top-30ish dynasty player for me, and could be awfully Javy Baez-y except without strikeouts (read: really, really good).

★ ★ ★ *2020 Top 101 Prospect* **#28** ★ ★ ★

2 Brendan McKay   LHP
Born: 12/18/95   Age: 24   Bats: L   Throws: L   Height: 6'2"   Weight: 212
Origin: Round 1, 2017 Draft (#4 overall)

The Report: After dominating the upper minors in the first half of 2019, McKay just barely qualifies for this list, having tossed 49 innings for the Rays. It was an uneven major-league debut for the polished lefty. His fastball actually ticked up in the majors, sitting 93-94 and touching 96. He spots it well to both sides, although there isn't a ton of wiggle. In the majors, he leaned heavily on his potential plus curveball. Uncle Chuck is a low-90s, sharp 1-7 breaker at its best, but will roll or flatten out some when he's spamming it. McKay mostly eschewed his change—which has had average projection in the past—for a fringy cutter against righties. He has an ideal frame and delivery for a starting pitcher, but his plus command didn't show up consistently, and McKay's fastball and cutter got punished in the zone by major league hitters.

We still list McKay as a two-way player, but it's fairly clear at this point that his future is on the mound. His arm got him to the majors faster than his bat could develop, but it was always a bit of a longshot that the offensive profile would play as a DH even with full-time hitting development. He may have some Michael Lorenzenish utility if the Rays want to get creative, but a solid number three starter is valuable enough on its own.

Variance: Low. McKay has about as much major-league experience as you can have while still being eligible for this list, and he was a polished lefty even in college. He needs to tighten up his command to hit this OFP, but there have always been positive markers there.

Mark Barry's Fantasy Take: McKay is a tricky one (there's the top-level analysis you came for). The lefty enjoyed some success strikeout-wise in a late-season cup of coffee, but didn't get a ton of swinging strikes, which could signal trouble for sustainability. Having said that, a hilariously low strand rate and a hilariously high BABIP wreaked havoc on his ERA, so we could see some positive regression on that front. It's unlikely McKay will be a star, but if the Rays allow him to log some innings, we could see a handful of SP3 seasons scattered on his otherwise around-average resume. I do not think we'll see much offense, so don't count on it.

★ ★ ★ *2020 Top 101 Prospect* **#30** ★ ★ ★

3
Shane Baz   RHP   OFP: 60   ETA: 2022
Born: 06/17/99   Age: 21   Bats: R   Throws: R   Height: 6'2"   Weight: 190
Origin: Round 1, 2017 Draft (#12 overall)

The Report: The trade with the Pirates that brought Baz to Tampa Bay in 2018 is looking more and more like highway robbery. Austin Meadows and Tyler Glasnow have already made their mark, and it looks as though Baz will do the same after a successful year with Low-A Bowling Green. The tall and slender righty has easy gas, pumping 96-98, and he locates the heat well in the upper half of the zone. Add a deceptive three-quarters arm slot and his fastball is a true swing-and-miss pitch. He does have a tendency to overthrow at times, which results in loss of command, but it doesn't seem to be a mechanical issue. Baz also employs a sharp, plus slider, sitting mid-80s and touching 88, featuring excellent tilt. That's a second out-pitch in his arsenal. A mid-80s changeup is a work in progress, but it shows some potential with solid arm-side fade. There is a lot to like in Baz's profile. He has quick arm action, he's athletic, and has already shown that he has an idea of how to pitch. The ceiling is quite high with his lethal fastball/slider combination alone.

Variance: High. With any young flame-thrower, the risk of future arm issues will always be present, and his shorter arm action adds to the injury risk. Additionally, he will need to start filling up the strike zone a little more to ease command concerns.

Mark Barry's Fantasy Take: Man, that Chris Archer trade is just the gift that keeps on giving (well, for the Rays, at least). If it's ceiling you seek, might I interest you in a little Baz? While McKay offers the stability of a high floor, Baz is all upside baby. His charitability has been troubling this season, dishing out a small village worth of free passes, but the improvement of his changeup as a legit third pitch has me dreaming on an SP2 flirting with that top tier of fantasy aces.

★ ★ ★ *2020 Top 101 Prospect* **#50** ★ ★ ★

4
Matthew Liberatore   LHP   OFP: 60   ETA: 2022
Born: 11/06/99   Age: 20   Bats: L   Throws: L   Height: 6'5"   Weight: 200
Origin: Round 1, 2018 Draft (#16 overall)

The Report: A first-round pick in 2018, Liberatore has quickly risen through the prospect ranks. The lefty throws from a high-three-quarters slot, creating excellent extension and downhill plane with his tall, wiry frame. He offers a four-pitch mix, although none are true swing-and-miss offerings currently. Liberatore's fastball sits 93-94 mph with occasional, slight tail and the command isn't there yet so hitters can square it up more than you'd like. His best pitch is an 11-6, upper-70s curveball that comes in on a high angle and features late bite. It has the makings of a potential plus pitch. A mid-80s changeup with hard dive also shows potential, but consistent feel and command still are issues. His fourth pitch is a below-average slider in the low 80s. Given his age and limited pro experience, Liberatore showed a lot of poise on the mound, which is a positive marker for his development. The profile isn't electric, but it offers potential along with a relatively high floor for a prep arm.

Variance: High. Without a true swing-and-miss pitch at the moment to lean heavily on, Liberatore will need to fine-tune his command at each step in the minors.

Mark Barry's Fantasy Take: No shots at Liberatore. He's a good, if not great, pitching prospect. I'm just a little concerned about the lack of strikeouts in the minors. He got a ton of groundballs in 2019, but his lack of a true swing-and-miss pitch doesn't bode well for his ability to be a strikeout asset in the big leagues. Sometimes these low-K, high-GB guys turn into Dallas Keuchel. Other times they're late-career Andrew Cashner. The boring and hedging answer is that Liberatore will probably wind up as something in the middle, with a Jalen Beeks-type future of bulking after an opener potentially in his future.

─────── ★ ★ ★ *2020 Top 101 Prospect* **#71** ★ ★ ★ ───────

5
Shane McClanahan   LHP   OFP: 60   ETA: 2021
Born: 04/28/97   Age: 23   Bats: L   Throws: L   Height: 6'1"   Weight: 200
Origin: Round 1C, 2018 Draft (#31 overall)

The Report: McClanahan teamed with fellow first-rounders Baz and Liberatore to anchor a formidable rotation in Bowling Green. But, while his teammates spent the entire summer in Kentucky, McClanahan breezed through two levels before finishing up in the Southern League. His fastball is electric, sitting in the high 90s with deception. It's the type of pitch that makes hitters uncomfortable. He features two secondaries, a 12-6 curve, and a change that sits in the high 80s. Neither is perfected yet. While he still struggles with consistency with the breaker, the curve can be a knee-buckler when he gets it right. On the mound, he's an extremely quick worker, with some moderate effort in the delivery. This causes him to get out of sync at times, and negatively impacts his command projection. The future might eventually be in the bullpen, but for now the Rays seem committed to using his high-ceiling arm in a starting role.

Variance: Medium. The lack of consistency in the secondaries and command are a concern, but the plus-plus fastball makes up for a lot.

Mark Barry's Fantasy Take: I am a very large fan of strikeouts. McLahahan punched out 154 dudes in 120 2/3 innings this season and has a premium, plus heater. If the breaker gets consistent, good lord, look out. In addition, while his former rotation-mates Baz and Liberatore topped out in Bowling Green, McLanahan made it to Double-A for four starts, making a 2020 big-league look more of a realistic possibility. Blah blah blah TINSTAAPP (I'm just as guilty of this by the way) blah blah. There's a bullpen risk, sure, but the pure upside makes McLanahan a fringe-101 guy at the very worst.

★ ★ ★ *2020 Top 101 Prospect* **#73** ★ ★ ★

6
Vidal Brujan   2B   OFP: 60   ETA: 2020
Born: 02/09/98   Age: 22   Bats: B   Throws: R   Height: 5'9"   Weight: 155
Origin: International Free Agent, 2014

The Report: It is hard to crack the top five in this organization, as illustrated well by Brujan, who earned two double-plus grades off a look last season. His speed is plus-plus out of the box as he accelerates quickly and reaches his top speed in a flash. It forces infielders to work quickly and helps him to get infield hits. The hit tool could be 70-grade. He shows quality bat speed and control of the barrel, rarely swinging and missing in our looks. Brujan works the whole field, attacks fastballs, recognizes offspeed and knows what he can swing at and drive. While he won't ever be known as a home-run hitter (we think, baseballs and such), there is enough strength here to hit a lot of doubles and triples.

Defensively, he has primarily played second and short, showing quality range and a quick first step. His hands are fringe and he has had troubles with his throwing accuracy, leading this author to speculate that he could see time in the outfield, where his speed would be a true asset.

Variance: Medium. The quality of the hit tool and speed gives him major-league value even if the defense forces a move to another position. Being the Rays, he might be playing elsewhere soon, especially since he is Rule 5 eligible.

Mark Barry's Fantasy Take: I'm not sure if you're aware of this, but steals are rare in fantasy, and in baseball writ large. Brujan is fast, oh so fast, not only stealing tons of bases, but stealing them relatively efficiently. Last season he paired the speed with a double-digit walk rate and slugged nearly .460. That's an Adalberto Mondesi-type, no-doubt top-30 dynasty guy. This year the walks took a step back, and he slugged under .400. The speed and contact rate still plays, to be sure, but if he doesn't at least feign power, that's more Mallex Smith—still valuable, but not unequivocally elite.

★ ★ ★ *2020 Top 101 Prospect* **#95** ★ ★ ★

7
Xavier Edwards   2B/SS   OFP: 55   ETA: Late 2021/Early 2022
Born: 08/09/99   Age: 20   Bats: B   Throws: R   Height: 5'10"   Weight: 175
Origin: Round 1, 2018 Draft (#38 overall)

The Report: Edwards has borderline elite, game-changing speed. That's the top line summary—and by this point in the report the dynasty players have already put him near the top of their draft boards—but he's not a mere burner. He has a potential plus hit tool as well. Edwards knows the zone well and sprays the ball line-to-line with his quick hands and wrists. The swing is not geared to elevate, and the power projection is well-below-average, but the speed should allow him to grab an extra base or two when he shoots one in to the gaps.

Edwards split his time between second and shortstop this year, but second base is his likely long term home due to fringy arm strength. The hands and actions work well on the right side of the infield, and he has good instincts on grounders, so while I'd consider handing him an outfield glove to see if the speed could play in center as well, he'd be above-average overall at the keystone if you just want to stick him there for 150 games a year. The lack of power projection or premium defensive position limits the upside in the profile a little bit, but the hit tool and speed give him a good shot to have some sort of a bench role even if the bat is a little light at the highest level. We think he will hit enough to play everyday though.

Variance: Medium. The athletic tools should get him to the majors, but hit-tool-driven profiles in A-ball aren't the safest.

Mark Barry's Fantasy Take: Edwards stole 34 bases in his first full season as a pro, and has yet to hit below .300. That's pretty much all you need to know, mostly because that's all there is. In today's fantasy landscape, that's still super useful, however, and in Edwards's case specifically, it makes him a top-50 dynasty prospect.

8 Greg Jones SS   OFP: 55   ETA: 2022
Born: 03/07/98 Age: 22 Bats: B Throws: R Height: 6'2" Weight: 175
Origin: Round 1, 2019 Draft (#22 overall)

The Report: Jones continued his torrid hitting with Hudson Valley after he was drafted from UNC Wilmington with the 22nd-overall pick in the 2019 draft. Jones has an exciting collection of tools ranging from his 70 or 80-grade speed (depending on the day) to his impressive bat control. The strikeouts were up from college, but that was more a result of being too patient at the plate, similar to what Yoan Moncada struggled with pre-2019. The swing is actually quite nice. It's flat but he generates above-average bat speed and regularly drives the ball to the gaps. The bat and barrel control are good enough where he could hit for 10-15 home runs if he had more loft in the swing. Defensively, he has the physical tools to be a regular at shortstop. The range is undoubtedly there, though the footwork can get messy and he occasionally rushes throws. The arm strength is fine, and the reports on his defense have improved over time. If he did have to move off shortstop, his speed could play well in center field. The collection of tools at either premium position means Jones's path to the bigs is clearer than most other prospects.

Variance: Medium. He can play up the middle and has some feel to hit, so Jones has a solid shot of having some sort of major league career.

Mark Barry's Fantasy Take: Though his name is a little boring, Jones's profile is anything but. Much like Brujan, Jones is a high-contact, high-speed guy, with plate discipline to boot. He currently hits for less power than a decent-hitting pitcher, so you can really only rely on him for a max of four categories. Even so, he's a top-150 fantasy prospect, for sure.

9. Ronaldo Hernandez C
OFP: 55 ETA: 2021
Born: 11/11/97 Age: 22 Bats: R Throws: R Height: 6'1" Weight: 185
Origin: International Free Agent, 2014

The Report: Hernandez was an infielder when the Rays originally signed him. They moved him behind the dish in his first pro season, so he has had a lot of work to do to learn the nuances of catching. The defensive part of his game is coming along, as he does show some aptitude for blocking and receiving, though he still lacks consistency in those areas. Hernandez has always had the arm to be successful, and he has made progress with his transfer and footwork to improve his overall catch-and-throw skills. With continued refinement, Hernandez should be able to develop into at least an average defensive catcher.

At the plate, Hernandez still shows flashes of plus raw power, but his approach leaves him struggling to get to that pop into games. He is a very aggressive hitter who makes a lot of contact, but he needs to learn to be more selective. He tends to swing at every pitch he can make contact with rather than being focused on those he can drive. Unsurprisingly, Hernandez is also very pull-oriented. The overall approach leaves him making too much weak contact. The foundational tools are there if he can find some patience and not be afraid to let his power play the other way at times.

Hernandez will face a tough test in Double-A and how he handles the offensive part of his development will make all the difference in determining his prospect trajectory.

Variance: High, especially given the work still remaining on defense.

Mark Barry's Fantasy Take: Though Hernandez is moving up from his 2018 spot on this list, it's hard to imagine anything other than a drop in his fantasy standing. He snagged seven bases without being caught, which is cool, but Hernandez hit just nine homers, down from 21 in 2018. That's less cool. Learning to catch is hard. Learning plate discipline is hard. Trying to learn them both at the same time: Priceless (wait that doesn't even make sense). Since fantasy catcher is still, and will likely always be, a barren wasteland, Hernandez is still one of the top-five catching prospects in fantasy, but his 2019 wasn't a step in the right direction.

10. Brent Honeywell Jr. RHP
OFP: 60 ETA:
Born: 03/31/95 Age: 25 Bats: R Throws: R Height: 6'2" Weight: 180
Origin: Round 2, 2014 Draft (#72 overall)

The Report: The backbone of these lists are our staff's live looks. You may be tired of us writing that by now. Usually there is a greater rhetorical point we are making, but in this case, it's a preamble to throwing up our hands. While rehabbing from Tommy John surgery this Summer, Honeywell fractured a bone in his elbow. There was no further ligament damage, but the former top-20 prospect hasn't thrown a pitch in a pro game in two years now. We've dealt with this situation before. Jameson Taillon was shut down during TJ rehab, but that was a hernia, and he's not exactly been a sterling example of pitcher health since then anyway. The comp for this kind of injury is Jeremy Hefner, who never pitched again after breaking his arm on rehab, although that injury necessitated a second surgery.

Like I wrote in the 2016 Annual for Taillon, I have no idea if this Honeywell ranking will look high or low in a year. But we have to put him somewhere. The rules are the rules.

Variance: Extreme. The stuff is front-of-the-rotation. He also might literally never pitch professionally again.

Mark Barry's Fantasy Take: I'm so mad ¯_(ツ)_/¯ got used for Honeywell before I had the chance. He's the ultimate lottery ticket where if you win, you get a stud, ace-level starter and if you lose you get punched in the face.

The Next Ten

11 Joe Ryan RHP
Born: 06/05/96 Age: 24 Bats: R Throws: R Height: 6'1" Weight: 185
Origin: Round 7, 2018 Draft (#210 overall)

The Report: Did the Rays do it again? Ryan comes aggressively to the plate with a three-quarters slot and smooth delivery. At 6-foot-1, Ryan isn't the most intimidating presence on the mound, but he is fairly consistent in his release and exudes supreme confidence throwing his dart of a fastball. The pitch has natural sink and projects for future plus command. It sits in the low 90s and has topped out at 96. The curveball comes in in the low 70s and flashes above-average. The shape isn't as tight as one may like at the moment, but used in combination with his impressive fastball it's an effective change of pace.

Ryan also has a cutter that's nothing to write home about yet, and a low-80s changeup that also needs work. But guess what? It's the Rays. As a traditional starter, this probably won't work, but as a mid-game three-to-four inning pitcher that fastball-curve mix would play.

Variance: High. Ryan is a thin four-pitch pitcher with two-and-a-half pitches at present.

Mark Barry's Fantasy Take: I kinda like this guy. Sure he might be a reliever. Sure he might be a tiny bit too old for High-A. Sure pumping low-90s fastballs as your primary pitch is probably better out of the bullpen. Wait, where was I? Ryan seems like the kind of guy that gets tossed into a spot start and then saves your season for like three months. It might not be until 2021, but a saved season is still a saved season. Additionally, it's hard to bet against a Cal State Stanislaus alum, because as we all know, nothing bad has ever come to a Stannis-ian.

12 Seth Johnson RHP
Born: 09/19/98 Age: 21 Bats: R Throws: R Height: 6'1" Weight: 200
Origin: Round 1, 2019 Draft (#40 overall)

From anonymity to a top-40 pick in the draft, Johnson went from a light-hitting JuCo shortstop to Campbell University No. 1 starter to legitimate pitching prospect in just over a year's time. You can see the former infielder's athleticism in the delivery, as he stays balanced over his front-side with easy effort in the arm action. Johnson is still very raw in terms of developing his pitches and learning to pitch, but with a fastball bumping 97-98 and the makings of a plus slider, there is a very talented base to build on. There were some durability concerns as the year wore on, and he came out of the bullpen for the Camels in the NCAA Tournament instead of starting. Building up a starter's endurance will be among the first tasks as he approaches his first full year in pro ball with the Rays.

13 Josh Lowe OF
Born: 02/02/98 Age: 22 Bats: L Throws: R Height: 6'4" Weight: 205
Origin: Round 1, 2016 Draft (#13 overall)

Going into the 2016 draft, Nate Lowe was referred to as the brother of Josh. Fast forward to the present day and now Josh is known as Nate Lowe's brother. That's mostly because of Nate's rather quick ascendance than the development of Josh, who could still end up being a better major leaguer. The younger Lowe oozes athleticism, tools and physicality, and seeing him in Arizona after a poor showing in 2018 reaffirmed the upside here. There are a lot of tools here: plus speed, plus raw pop, plus throwing arm and quality outfield defense. The power improved in 2019, as he added strength over last year and drove the ball to all fields more effectively. He still struggles against better breaking stuff and might always be vulnerable against lefties, lowering his overall ceiling. Still, when there are this many tools in the profile, I will always be a believer.

14 Nick Schnell OF
Born: 03/27/00 Age: 20 Bats: L Throws: R Height: 6'3" Weight: 180
Origin: Round 1C, 2018 Draft (#32 overall)

Another toolsy athlete with upside. Schnell keeps his hands low pre-pitch and slightly moves his load up to get to the baseball. It's not a rip-through-the-ball swing, but it's pretty clean. Nothing is really too loud at that plate, but he probably projects as a 50 hit, 50 power guy. Still raw as hell, but a Ross-Adolph-type profile with a touch more speed and a better arm fits this 2018 first-round selection.

15 Lucius Fox SS
Born: 07/02/97 Age: 22 Bats: B Throws: R Height: 6'1" Weight: 180
Origin: International Free Agent, 2015

Fox projects for little power from either side of the plate with a pretty weak swing. It has a one-handed release with a toe tap and a bit of a timid approach—30 game power with very little room for projection. However, the swing is not carrying Fox in the majors (or minors for that matter). The Bahamanian is a 70 runner and possesses high-end athleticism. He still looks raw in pretty much all facets of the game except on the basepaths— but there is some projectability in the game and the glove. We *pretty* much know what he is by now, but if the athleticism allows him to get to above-average at shortstop, he could be a fringe starter.

16 Anthony Banda LHP
Born: 08/10/93 Age: 26 Bats: L Throws: L Height: 6'2" Weight: 225
Origin: Round 10, 2012 Draft (#335 overall)

Banda stepped back on a complex-league mound a shade over a year after his 2018 Tommy John surgery. He rehabbed at a fairly quick pace, and the results were good enough to find himself back in the majors after rosters expanded in September. Banda was mostly fastball/slider/change in 2019. The fastball can hit 93-94 with regularity and there's some deception, but not a ton of movement. The slider is averageish as well. It's a firm, mid-80s offering that he can front door to lefties or backfoot to righties, but it can lack ideal depth. The change remains a bit of a work in progress. He's still close enough to his surgery date that you can hope for the stuff to tick back up a bit more, but he's also major-league-ready enough to be a useful utility arm for the 2020 Rays.

17 JJ Goss RHP
Born: 12/25/00 Age: 19 Bats: R Throws: R Height: 6'3" Weight: 185
Origin: Round 1, 2019 Draft (#36 overall)

Goss isn't your traditional big ol' Day One Texas prep arm. He's a projectable 6-foot-3, mostly because he's pretty doggone skinny, but he generates average fastball velocity at present from a short, quick arm action. There might be more in the tank there as well given the present frame. Goss has a very advanced low-80s breaking ball for a prep arm, and the requisite developing changeup. It's going to be interesting to see how he grows into his body, but there are positive markers in his delivery to stick as a starter if the third pitch develops.

18 Kevin Padlo 3B
Born: 07/15/96 Age: 23 Bats: R Throws: R Height: 6'2" Weight: 205
Origin: Round 5, 2014 Draft (#143 overall)

After two middling campaigns in A-ball where Padlo struggled to get his raw power into games, a swing adjustment may have unlocked something for him in the upper minors. Padlo starts with his hands back now, almost at a full arm bar, and explodes at pitches with loft. You have to be pretty strong to pull that off, but Padlo looks the part in short sleeves, and he smashed 21 home runs in 110 upper minors games. The quality of contact isn't always going to be great and he'll pop a fair bit of high fastballs up, but he has a strong enough approach to perhaps make the offensive profile work overall. It might look a bit like post-peak Todd Frazier, although the glove at third base is more average than plus. Doing enough damage on contact with this kind of swing can be tricky against major league arms, so there's a wide range of uncertainty on the hit tool, but Padlo is very much a hitter of his times. Well, assuming the ball stays juiced.

19 Niko Hulsizer   OF
Born: 02/01/97   Age: 23   Bats: R   Throws: R   Height: 6'2"   Weight: 225
Origin: Round 18, 2018 Draft (#554 overall)

As an 18th-round draft choice out of Morehead State in 2018, Hulsizer wasn't on many prospect radars to begin the year. Then he was traded to the Rays, and being traded to the Rays seems to guarantee improvements these days. Hulsizer is a tank—from top to bottom he is as solidly built as they come. He's an average runner with an average glove and an average arm, but his power is very much not average. The raw is an easy 70. He's as strong as an ox, shows plus bat speed, and generates loft from his swing plane. According to the Rancho Cucamonga Quakes one of his home runs left the bat at 116 mph.

Hulsizer's hit tool might reach average if everything goes right developmentally, and if that happens you have a plus regular. He shows good pitch recognition and a nice approach at the plate. Still, at present there are some issues, the biggest of which is significant swing-and-miss. I always find it promising when hitters with swing-and-miss issues can still earn walks at a healthy clip, and Hulsizer definitely does that (12.9 percent walk rate). For as bulky as he is, he's a good athlete which should make reaching his OFP more likely than average. He is an immediate eye-catcher on the field and if he continues to put up the numbers he did in 2019 expect him to fly up prospect rankings at midseason.

20 Simon Rosenblum-Larson   RHP
Born: 02/11/97   Age: 23   Bats: R   Throws: R   Height: 6'3"   Weight: 202
Origin: Round 19, 2018 Draft (#570 overall)

The Harvard draftee has a fastball that sits 88-91 with plenty of running action. The delivery features a big drop and drive. The arm slot is sidearm, but it doesn't feature the shoulder drop in the back that traditional sidearms and submariners have. His upper-70s slider features incredible sweeping action, and plays well off the fastball that moves arm-side. The red flag here is the command, as

Rosenblum-Larson really slings it, causing both the fastball and slider to miss outside the zone too often. He's the type of arm you throw out there if you really need a strikeout, but have to pull him quickly if the command isn't there that day.

Personal Cheeseball

PC **Drew Strotman   RHP**
Born: 09/03/96   Age: 23   Bats: R   Throws: R   Height: 6'3"   Weight: 195
Origin: Round 4, 2017 Draft (#109 overall)

I liked Strotman coming out of the 2017 draft as a four-pitch small college guy who mixed his stuff pretty well, even if he lacked a standout, or even above-average offering. Tommy John surgery cost him most of 2018 and 2019, but he's back on the mound now and was working at the upper end of his velocity range in the AFL. That's a borderline plus fastball, but it doesn't move a ton and the command projection is only average. Strotman also has two potentially average breaking balls, and a below-average change. He's lost a fair bit of development time to injury already, but during his time on the shelf, the Rays have popularized a role for this kind of pitcher as a bulk innings guy behind an opener. So he's got that going for him.

Low Minors Sleeper

LMS **Neraldo Catalina   RHP**
Born: 06/21/00   Age: 20   Bats: R   Throws: R   Height: 6'6"   Weight: 202
Origin: International Free Agent, 2018

Much of this list is an ode to the Rays' pro scouting and player development teams. We don't want to puff them up too too much, but it was kind of unfair that they were allowed to trade with the Mets this season. Catalina—the return for roughly two months of Wilmer Font—was a $150k, overage, but still quite projectable, IFA that popped some in Extended Spring Training. The 6-foot-6 righty sits mid-90s, touching higher, with a potentially average curve. He's a two-pitch guy at present, but there's a lot of raw material to work with here. He would have made the Mets list comfortably.

Top Talents 25 and Under (as of 4/1/2020)

1. Wander Franco
2. Austin Meadows
3. Brendan McKay
4. Shane Baz
5. Brandon Lowe
6. Matthew Liberatore

7. Willy Adames
8. Vidal Brujan
9. Nate Lowe
10. Greg Jones

The fact that Franco ranks ahead of a 25-year-old outfielder coming off an All-Star season speaks to the type of generational talent he's projected to become. Meadows is no slouch himself, of course, as his 135 DRC+ ranked 18th in the majors, tied with top-three MVP finisher Marcus Semien. His power-speed combo should be something the Rays can rely on for the next half-decade at least, and while he won't be confused for Mookie Betts in right field, he can hold his own out there and masquerade in center if the situation called for it. Brandon Lowe acclimated himself well in his first extended look at playing time and also made the All-Star team, at which point he suffered a shin injury that shut him down for most of the rest of the season. When he did play, the swing change that landed him on the radar a year ago played up and he exhibited solid power that more than made up for the swing-and-miss in his approach. It was an impressive enough season to boost him ahead of Adames, whose 3.8 WARP season was thanks almost entirely to his glove which FRAA said was the best—or at least the most consistent—in all of baseball. Adames's bat was unreliable, but the power many hoped he'd develop was there, at least in this juiced-up-baseball world. The only other player not eligible for the prospect list to grace our Top 10 is Lowe No. 2, Nate, whose TTO routine translated to the majors in a 50-game audition—40 percent of his plate appearances ended in either a home run, walk, or strikeout. Tampa had a glut of 1B/DH types on their roster in 2019—Ji-Man Choi, Yandy Diaz, Jesus Aguilar—but he should get an extended look if and when circumstances surrounding the position change.

Part 3: Featured Articles

The Baseball Is Juiced (Again)

Robert Arthur

This article originally appeared at Baseball Prospectus on April 5, 2019.

It started when the normally reliable Chris Sale got lit up for three homers by the Mariners in the Red Sox's season opener. It was part of a record number of taters that flew on Opening Day, as starters from Sale to Zack Greinke were taken deep by the handful. Then Christian Yelich hit a home run in each of his first four games, tying yet another MLB record, this one for consecutive games with a dinger to start a season.

It didn't take long for fans and players to begin whispering and tweeting about the baseballs being juiced again. It's early yet for us to come to any definitive conclusion about the 2019 season, but preliminary data shows that the baseball has returned to its aerodynamic peak. Whether that means this season will smash home run records like 2017 did remains to be seen.

Before home run explosion over the last few years, no one worried too much about the baseball's air resistance. While MLB and Rawlings (the company that manufactures the official baseballs) kept track of dozens of metrics to make sure that the ball was consistent from month to month, they didn't measure drag.

But drag is incredibly important in determining how likely a hitter is to knock one out of the park. As baseballs become more aerodynamic, they travel further given a certain initial velocity. A deep fly ball that might have been caught at the warning track can instead go into the first row of the stands. A three percent change in drag coefficient can work to add about five feet to a well-hit fly ball, which can in turn increase home runs league wide by an astounding 10-15 percent.

It's possible to measure the aerodynamics of the baseball using the pitch-tracking radars currently in place in each MLB ballpark. By calculating the loss of speed from when the pitch is released to when it crosses the plate, you can directly measure the drag coefficient on the baseball. I first wrote about the role of decreasing drag in boosting home runs in 2017, and MLB's commission of scientists and statisticians later confirmed that the more aerodynamic baseballs in use that year were largely to blame for the spike in home runs. The same commission rejected some alternate hypotheses, like rising temperatures and a league-wide boost in launch angle pushing more balls over the fence.

The current era has featured some large fluctuations in drag coefficient, leading to first an explosion in 2016 and 2017, and then a dialing back of homers last year. Curious about the record-breaking home run tallies in the last few days, I used the same methodology to measure the aerodynamics of the baseballs so far in 2019.

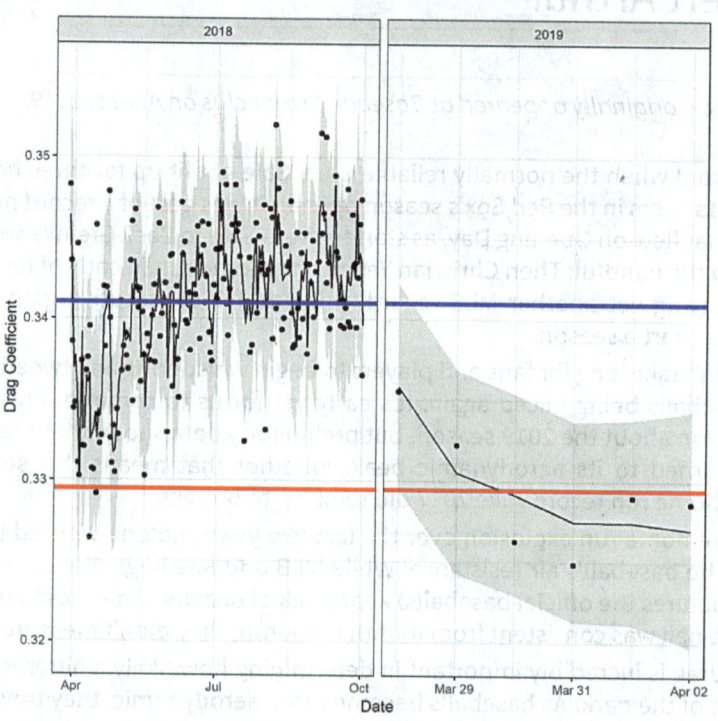

We're only a week into the 2019 season, but the drag numbers so far are among the lowest recorded in the last calendar year. With apologies for gory math, the current 2019 season average drag coefficient (the red line) would be below the 95 percent credible interval (the shaded area) for about nine-tenths of the 2018 season. (I used a Bayesian Random Walk model implemented in INLA to calculate these credible intervals, averaging the drag numbers in each game and adjusting for park.)

There were only a handful of six-day stretches in 2018 that had drag numbers below what we're seeing now, and most were in late June and early July. All of this means that 2019's data so far is quite a bit different than what we saw through most of last year.

These drag coefficients factor out the effects of temperature and air density, so they aren't a product of April cold. However, the numbers could be deceptive if the radars used to track pitches have changed from year to year. I consulted with some experts within baseball who were not aware of any specific modifications to the radar this year that could produce this pattern, but it's an important caveat of which to be aware.

On the one hand, it's only been six days, and we don't quite have the statistical basis to say that these drag coefficients are unprecedented compared to 2018. On the other hand, we've witnessed about 5,000 fastballs so far this season, so it's not as if our sample size is small. At least so far, the baseball has played like it's much more aerodynamic than it was last year. In fact, the current drag coefficient is really only comparable to 2017, when the baseballs were more aerodynamic than they had been in at least a decade.

It's not just fancy radar tracking indicating that the baseball is flying through the air more easily. The current number of home runs per game (as of this writing) is the highest it's been since the heady days of 2017, the year that teams and players broke dinger-related records everywhere you looked. That's especially remarkable considering that we're in what is typically the coldest part of the regular season, when lower temperatures and higher winds tend to suppress offense and keep balls in the air within the park. Comparing only from April to April, this year's rate of home runs per fly ball is even a little bit higher than it was in 2017.

With that said, the current measurements are no guarantee that 2019 will be another year of record-shattering homer hitting. The trouble with the drag measurements is that they are not consistent from June to August, from week to week, or even sometimes from day to day. Whether because of natural manufacturing variation or differences in the underlying supplies of cowhide and thread that go into the baseballs, drag has a tendency to fluctuate up and down over the course of a year. So the homers that fly in the first week of April wouldn't necessarily clear the fence a week later.

It's possible that this one-week drop in drag coefficient subsides and the baseball returns to its 2018 levels. On the other hand, it's almost equally probable that the ball becomes even more slippery and flies ever farther. Either way, it's clear that the baseball's air resistance is something to keep an eye on for the remainder of the 2019 season.

—*Robert Arthur is an author of Baseball Prospectus.*

The Moral Hazard of Playing It Safe

Craig Goldstein

This article originally appeared at Baseball Prospectus on August 6, 2019.

A couple days prior to the trade deadline, amidst a sea of tranquility posing as the lead up to the trade deadline, Bob Nightengale took to Twitter. Nightengale, who was probably wearing his pants backwards at the time, tweeted that MLB GMs were coming around on the idea that the unified trade deadline should be moved back from July 31 to August 15, so they could better assess their positions in the standings and whether they should buy or sell. To which I said:

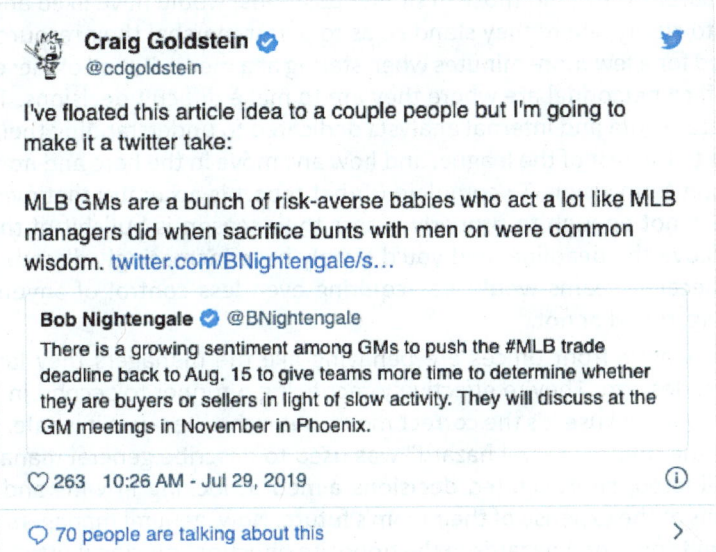

This might strike some as reductive and churlish. And it might be that, but it isn't really wrong, either. Jeff Quinton wrote a great piece discussing the environmental factors that enable front offices to avoid risk without upsetting the apple cart within their own fanbases. I don't believe that it goes far enough, however. His article gives us the proper framework through which to understand why these behaviors have been allowed to seep into front offices throughout the league. Understanding the reasons behind these actions are different from excusing them, though, and GMs should not be let off the hook for their non-competitive approach to the trade deadline (much less the offseason).

⚾   ⚾   ⚾

It's fair to say that fans as a group have rarely, if ever, been pro-player. It is also fair to say that in the time during and following the Moneyball revolution, the pendulum swung from fans who cared intensely about winning in the moment (and thus might be intolerant of a rebuilding approach) to fans who supported building a team that could compete throughout multiple seasons, viewing the playoffs as a crapshoot, with the thought that getting multiple bites at the apple was a better approach than taking a bigger bite in any one season.

There's nothing wrong with that approach, and I still find merit in that argument. However, it seems that the pendulum has swung too far in that direction. Teams are overvaluing some of the individual factors that make themselves long-term contenders rather than attempting to seize a championship when given the opportunity. It's a difficult needle to thread.

And surely, they (and those in similar positions) would have liked another two weeks to clarify where they stand so as to better marshal their resources. We've all asked for a few more minutes when staring at a menu. But all of these GMs and front office personnel are where they are to make difficult decisions. They have proprietary data and internal analysts dedicated to understanding their position relative to the rest of the league, and how any move in the here and now impacts their long-term vision. To complain (if that report is accurate) that over half the season is not enough to properly assess their season is bullshit of the highest order. Move the deadline, and you'd simply have increasingly discounted trade offers because teams would be acquiring even less control of anyone they're acquiring, rental or not.

Major league front offices are behaving like the managers they lampooned two decades ago. They're effectively sacrificing a runner to second in the ninth inning—not because it's the correct move, but rather because it is safe. It used to be that the phrase "moral hazard" was used to describe general managers who made ill-fated, short-sighted decisions aimed at locking in wins and securing their jobs at the expense of their team's future. Now, general managers are guilty of committing moral hazards in the opposite direction, playing it utterly safe and terrified of becoming scapegoats.

In lieu of bold action, they opt to pussyfoot around a current window of contention, choosing instead to play the long game and stack up years of control like they're blocks in a game of Jenga. GMs pass on signing quality players in free agency because the back-end of the deal might look bad, and because they might be able to squeeze out 70 percent of the production from a player who costs a tenth as much. That's a safer investment, too, because it's also hard to prove a negative—it's impossible to prove that Manny Machado would make the Mets a playoff team in 2019-2020, but it's easy to say that the back half of Robinson Cano's contract sucks. Owners, who rule over GM's jobs, are also humans with human brain processes that will always make the so-called albatross contract uglier than the road not taken.

These days, GMs are remembered for the bad deals they make and the surplus value they generate, not the acquisition of expensive, necessary talents that meet their market worth (or fall slightly short while still providing significant on-field value). And front offices know that one or two expensive misfires can cost them their jobs, no matter how many good deals they make.

No front office exemplifies this ethos more than the Toronto Blue Jays. General Manager Ross Atkins had this to say following the Blue Jays underwhelming trade deadline:

This is by no means the first time that an executive will cite years of control to justify their actions, which is often just another way of saying "don't look at what we got, look at how much we got of it." Atkins touts quantity to elide the discussion of quality—either, that of the players acquired, or those given up. Remember: the other teams presumably value years of control, too.

Atkins also had some thoughts to offer regarding free agents back in early 2018:

This ignores, of course, whether the player can create enough value in the front end of a contract to justify the longer term of a deal, and the decline that often occurs in the back end. It also ignores whether the player can fill a need the team requires and put them in a position to compete for and win a championship. But as teams seemingly avoid contention at all, where they might end up having to consider and later justify some of these tough decisions, we still see risk-averse approaches.

Anthony Fenech's article on two trades that recently extended GM Al Avila didn't make got at this issue rather well:

> Passing on those deals was defensible: Both players had yet to break out and trading [Michael] Fulmer—a pitcher who appeared to be a future ace, no matter his injury concerns—would have taken serious gumption, opening Avila up to strong criticism.

Avoiding strong criticism is something each of us can understand as a motivation, but the avoidance of criticism only matters if that criticism is valid. In Fulmer's case, shoving his injury concerns aside affects not only the years that the team controls him (he is currently missing a full season due to Tommy John surgery) but also the quality of those seasons, as his knee and elbow injuries combined to dampen his effectiveness even when healthy enough to pitch. But it was easy to present the then-current image of Fulmer as a top of the rotation pitcher who the team had under its domain for the next five seasons as something to build around. The status quo isn't nearly as often second-guessed as a decision that disrupts it.

⚾ ⚾ ⚾

MLB GMs are risk-averse to a fault. They are ivy-educated and consulting firm-approved, and yet they can't seem to avoid leaving wins on the table in their all-consuming lust for a non-existent $/WAR championship. They are supposed to zig when everyone else zags, and not merely pay lip service to the idea of zigging through a calculated PR plan built on convincing the fan base their approach is novel when it actually apes most of their competitors. Instead they've become far more concerned with making safe, accepted-by-the-new-common-wisdom decisions, such that our prior understanding of what a moral hazard is has become inverted.

I can't blame them entirely, and not only because of the reasons that Quinton illuminated in his article, but also because of the damage wrought by the introduction of the second wild card (WC2) spot. MLB's desire to have more teams in playoff contention has sparked anti-competitive behavior. Teams know now that they do not need to swing big as they assemble their roster because there is a good chance that a mediocre team can either catch fire and capture a division, or muddle along until they back into the WC2.

Simultaneously, the one-game playoff has neutered the WC1, putting an entire season on the flip of a coin like some sort of baseball-obsessed Anton Chigurh. While the one-game playoff makes sense as a way to increase the value of winning a division, it also means that if a front office doesn't like its chances of overcoming a behemoth like the Dodgers or Astros in the offseason, they have few incentives to chase glory. Similarly, the relative inaction in the NL Central at the trade deadline—despite a wide open division—can be explained by the idea that any high-variance investment could still result in only a wild card (or worse) result, given the mere two months left in the season to make an impact.

⚾ ⚾ ⚾

As stated at the top, we should not confuse reasons for excuses. The implementation of the second wild card is just one of many environmental factors that influence how each front office operates. I am convinced that it is one of the larger factors, but I am also convinced that organizations need to shed the yoke of "efficiency at all costs" so that they can instead pursue competition, as the spirit of the game intends. Until they do, we're all deadline losers.

—*Craig Goldstein is an author of Baseball Prospectus.*

Index of Names

Adames, Willy	26	Jones, Greg	93, 108
Alvarado, José	56	Kiermaier, Kevin	34
Alvarez, Roberto	100	Kittredge, Andrew	72
Anderson, Nick	58	Liberatore, Matthew	105
Arozarena, Randy	88	Lowe, Brandon	36
Banda, Anthony	96, 112	Lowe, Josh	100, 111
Baz, Shane	97, 105	Lowe, Nate	38
Beeks, Jalen	60	Margot, Manuel	40
Bonifacio, Emilio	100	Martínez, José	42
Brosseau, Michael	28	McClanahan, Shane	99, 106
Brujan, Vidal	89, 107	McKay, Brendan	74, 94, 104
Castillo, Diego	62	Meadows, Austin	44
Catalina, Neraldo	114	Milner, Hoby	101
Chirinos, Yonny	64	Morton, Charlie	76
Choi, Ji-Man	30	O'Grady, Brian	100
Covey, Dylan	66	Padlo, Kevin	100, 112
Cozens, Dylan	100	Perez, Michael	100
Davis, Johnny	100	Poche, Colin	78
Díaz, Yandy	32	Renfroe, Hunter	46
Doxakis, John	101	Richards, Trevor	80
Drake, Oliver	68	Robertson, Daniel	48
Edwards, Xavier	90, 107	Roe, Chaz	82
Fairbanks, Peter	101	Rosenblum-Larson, Simon	113
Fox, Lucius	100, 112	Ryan, Joe	101, 110
Franco, Wander	91, 103	Sanders, Phoenix	101
Glasnow, Tyler	70	Schnell, Nick	111
Goss, J.J.	101, 112	Slegers, Aaron	101
Hernandez, Ronaldo	92, 109	Smith, Kevan	50
Honeywell Jr., Brent	98, 109	Snell, Blake	84
Hulsizer, Niko	100, 113	Strotman, Drew	114
Johnson, Seth	101, 111	Tsutsugoh, Yoshitomo	95

Tampa Bay Rays 2020

Wendle, Joey 52
Whitley, Garrett 100
Yarbrough, Ryan 86
Zunino, Mike 54